AF540486

Competency Framework for Human Resources Management

BY THE SAME AUTHOR

- — Governance and Management of Technical Institutions
- — Management of Competency Based Learning
- — Academic Audit
- — सीखने की विधियाँ (Learning Methods)

ABOUT THE AUTHOR

Dr. B.L. Gupta is Professor in Management at National Institute of Technical Teachers Training and Research, Bhopal. He completed B. E. in Civil Engineering in the year 1982 from SGSITS, Indore. He completed LL.B. from The College of Law and Legal Aid, Shahdol in the year 1988. Then he completed Master of Technical Education in the year 1992 and Ph.D. in 2002 from Technical Teachers' Training Institute, Bhopal. Professor Gupta has 27 years of experience in the field of teaching, training, research and consultancy. He is trained in Great Britain. He has received training from well-known personalities of the country. He has conducted more than 460 management development programmes for various clients such as teachers of technical institutions, trainers and managers of industries. He has guided more than 15 theses in the field of technical education and management of industries. He has published more than 50 papers in national and international journals. He has developed variety of print and non-print instructional material for teachers, managers, officers and employees of various organisations. He is a visiting faculty for a number of training institutions of repute. He has worked on various World Bank Assisted Projects. Earlier to this book he has written seventeen books.

Competency Framework for

Human Resources Management

B.L. Gupta

Professor, Management

National Institute of Technical Teachers' Training and Research, Shamla Hills, Bhopal-462002

badrilalgupta72@gmail.com

CONCEPT PUBLISHING COMPANY PVT. LTD.

NEW DELHI-110059

ISBN-13: 978-81-8069-738-8 (HB)

First Published 2011

Published and Printed by

Concept Publishing Company Pvt. Ltd.
Regd. Office:
A/15-16, Commercial Block, Mohan Garden
New Delhi-110059 (India)
Phones : 25351460, 25351794, *Fax* : 091-11-25357109
Email : publishing@conceptpub.com
Website: www.conceptpub.com

Editorial Office:
H-13, Bali Nagar, New Delhi-110 015, India.

Cataloging in Publication Data--Courtesy: D.K. Agencies (P) Ltd. <docinfo@dkagencies.com>

Gupta, B. L. (Badrilal), 1960-
Competency framework for human resources management / B.L. Gupta.
p. cm.
Includes bibliographical references (p.) and index.
ISBN 9788180697388

1. Personnel management. 2. Employee competitive behavior. I. Title.

DDC 658.3 22

Preface

For long the corporate sector has been searching for sound base for managing human resources but using traditional approaches. In the past decade some significant work on competency framework has been done in selected companies and government organizations. However, requisite literature was not available. To fulfil this need of the corporate world and government departments seemed to be the need of the time. Hence, the author considered it necessary to pen such a book.

This book particularly addresses the long felt needs of human resources (HR) manager responsible for competency based human resources management. It also addresses the needs of the industry, students, parents, statutory body, accreditation agency, and policy makers related to competency based human resources management. It will enable the HR managers to plan, design, implement and evaluate the competency based human resources management.

The author has used the relevant information from various disciplines, without defining and describing the concepts and principles. The readers are suggested to refer the relevant literature if they have further interest in related disciplines of human resources management. Based on the long experience of the author in the field of human resources management, many concepts, principles, models, procedures, tools, techniques and strategies necessary for managing competency framework and human resources have been suggested in this book. It is for the readers to exploit the full potential of this book. The approach here is not to rename the traditional human resources management as competency framework for managing human resources but it is completely new, different and unique.

The book is not intended to point out the strengths and weaknesses of current human resources management practices of corporate sector. However, along with the useful inputs, enough guidelines to develop and implement each concept and ample activities with references to competency framework are provided in this book. It is left to the readers to use the activities and diagnose the strengths and weaknesses of the human resources management practices with reference to competency framework.

Since the author has a long experience of designing, implementing and evaluating HR processes for technical education systems, government departments and corporate sector the book reflects the views expressed in various training programmes and other fora. This book also includes the suggestions expressed by the industry and significant stakeholders. In this context, the author records acknowledgement to the participants of various training programmes and industry personnel whose opinions, suggestions and ideas helped the author to conceptualize various models and strategies to publish this much needed book.

The author sincerely records acknowledgement to the Chairman and members of Board of Governors, Director and the faculty members of National Institute of Technical Teachers' Training and Research, Bhopal for their cooperation.

B.L. Gupta

Acknowledgements

This book on 'competency framework for human resources management' is the outcome of many precedent training experiences and research studies conducted in past. I wish to record my sincere thanks to following persons :

Ex Principals and Directors of National Institute of Technical Teachers' Training and Research, Bhopal for providing opportunities to get international exposure;

Dr. Vijay K. Agrawal, Director, National Institute of Technical Teachers' Training and Research, Bhopal;

Prof. (Mrs.) M. Saxena, Dr. Joshua Earnest and Dr. R.B. Shivagunde for sharing ideas on topics of common interest;

The research scholars and their guides for conducting the research studies on topics related to their interest;

My colleagues at National Institute of Technical Teachers' Training and Research, Bhopal for openly sharing the experiences;

Library staff of National Institute of Technical Teachers' Training and Research, Bhopal;

My father Shri Shriniwas Gupta and mother Mrs. Sushila Gupta for sharing everything. My wife Mrs. Suman Gupta, sons Kumar Gandharva, Kumar Gaurva, and my niece Swati Suneria and Meera Farkya for supporting me during writing work; and

Shri Ashok Mittal, Concept Publishing Company Pvt. Ltd., New Delhi for publishing the book.

Contents

List of Figures

List of Formats

How to Read This Book

This book on *Competency Framework for Human Resources Management is* written which can be read in any way the reader wants, depending on his/her interest. The book is equally useful for the new as well as experienced HR managers. In totality, it deals with paradigm shift required from traditional human resources management to competency based human resources management. The whole book is divided in 9 chapters.

Chapter 1 describes competency. Chapter 2 describes competency framework. Chapter 3 describes process of competency framework development. Chapter 4 describes tools and techniques for competency framework development. Chapter 5 describes assessment of competency. Chapter 6 describes competency based recruitment. Chapter 7 describes competency based training. Chapter 8 describes competency based performance review and Chapter 9 describes role of Human Resource managers.

The beginning of each chapter informs the readers about the *learning objectives* that will be achieved by him/her. If the learning needs of the readers match with the learning outcomes they must sincerely read the chapter. If they already know about the contents of the chapter they are suggested to undertake the *activities for the HR managers* for understanding the application of the contents in the chapter. Based on the difficulty level of activities the readers may refer to the matter presented in that chapter and others.

Each chapter also contains *figures* which shows the highlights and actions useful for assessment. The experienced and learned readers can directly read the matter presented in the summary. If they find any comprehension difficulty they can read related matter further explained and also illustrated in figures shown in certain places.

The book also contains *guidelines*, which can be followed while working on competency framework development. Guidelines are stated in positive way describing what to do and what not to do. The guidelines, if used, they can certainly enhance the effectiveness and efficiency of the competency framework development process. The guidelines are suggestive and not prescriptive.

Formats are given towards the end of chapters to apply the concepts, principles, models and practices or assess the current practices. In fact, formats help the HR managers in following the theory holistically. Formats help readers to recall the previously learnt theory. Formats are the link between theory and practice.

Activities for HR managers given at the end of chapters are useful in applying the learning, mastering the theory of competency framework development and using it for human resources management activities and reviewing the current practices of human resources management in the organization. It provides an opportunity for applying the learning of competency in real life situation. The readers are suggested to complete the activities after reading a particular chapter. The readers are suggested to interact on the output of completion of *activity for HR managers* with their colleagues. This approach would develop insight in using competency framework for managing human resources.

'Review questions' are given at the end of each chapter. These questions provide an opportunity to self-check the various dimensions of competency framework and human resources management. These questions will certainly compel the readers to think and apply the learning outcomes of this book.

Towards the end of this book *glossary of terms* is given for a better understanding of the book. Glossary defines the major terms used in the book. Readers are suggested to refer to the glossary whenever they find a new term while reading a particular chapter.

Wish you all the best with a request to mail your valuable suggestions for improving the contents and presentation of the book. The readers are also requested to share their experiences and case studies.

1

Competency

LEARNING OBJECTIVES

After reading this chapter the readers will be able to :

- Describe the changes taking place in external environment.
- State the need and importance of use of competency for human resources management.
- Explain the meaning of competency.
- Describe the concept of competency.
- Compare various definitions of competency.
- State the features of competencies.
- Classify the competencies on various parameters.
- State the sources of deriving competencies.
- Check the quality of competency statement.

1. Introduction

The developments taking place in every field have affected methods of carrying out the business. Every organization is promoting *professional* way of working to produce and deliver the goods and services. Organizations are facing unprecedented change, competition and uncertainty in the business. The developments are compelling them to renovate, innovate and continuously improve quality of products and services. This pressure of continuous change is pressing them to employ, retain, and develop professionals who can maintain the pace with the change and developments. Now they cannot afford to employ the persons and develop them on the job gaining experiences over a long period of time to perform professionally.

The organizations are intending to employ and retain *fast learners* and adopters in changing business. They are looking for the persons who can develop altogether new and different competencies in them in shortest possible time. The fast growth and development in the satellite technology, electronic media, and internet has significantly affected the business of every organizations. Now they are forced to integrate technology with their business.

In the competitive world the whole concept of *human resources management (HRM)* has changed significantly. The HR processes are required to provide technically competent professionals for all the core processes of the organization. Here the word professional is very important in the sense that professionals are required to satisfy and *delight* the customer in the competitive, changing, and challenging world of work. They are required to work in uncertainty, recession, fluctuating market, diverse culture, and different environment. They are required to work to long hours and without tension, stress, and anxiety. They are required to satisfy customers as well as *stakeholders*.

The definition of professionalism has changed over the years and still it is in fluid because the whole world is changing very fast. In the changing world of work it is very difficult to predict the status of the profession. The concern for safety and conserving environment has also increased significantly. The laws governing all the professions are being modified to control and regulate the unwanted and undesirable act of the companies.

In order to maintain and sustain professionalism in the organization, HR department is required to put sincere efforts from micro level to meta level to cope up with changing expectations of the external customers. There is a need to bring *professional approach* in the functioning of the organization then only it can think of producing six sigma quality products and services.

Professionally managed HR processes can only sustain and develop professionalism. Not to say that HR processes are not being designed and implemented professionally but there is a need of using professional approach based on competency framework which is scientific, objective, measurable and relevant in today's context. Along with core competencies the professionals are required to develop variety of professional competencies. An indicative list of significant professional competencies is given below :

Professional Competencies

- Accept challenges of the business and role,
- Take risk for grabbing the opportunity beneficial to the business,

- Work in teams to produce synergy in performance,
- Learn new competencies quickly to develop others,
- Solve complex problems professionally,
- Take effective decisions for the benefit of the organization,
- Negotiate with the suppliers, partners and other stakeholders for the benefit of the business of the organization,
- Collaborate with stakeholders, research organizations and resource institutions for mutual benefit,
- Network with different centres of excellence for designing and implementing different innovations,
- Work in uncertain situations to achieve the goals,
- Predict the future situations to take the advantage of the opportunities and minimize the threats,
- Visualize the whole on the basis of available data,
- Accept *accountability* for individual roles,
- Manage change for improving the quality of products and services,
- Cope up with changing and uncertain situations,
- Influence the customers for various purposes,
- Conduct research for developing new products, services and design projects for quick response to changing expectations of external and internal customers,
- Adjust in new culture,
- Adopt in different environment,
- Learn new and different competencies for self-development, and
- Forget fast the old competencies, etc.

Not to say that all the competencies listed here will require to be developed in all the employees but this is the need of the day. Considering the nature of the business more competencies can be added or deleted from the list.

There is a fast change in technology and way of working in the professional world. Companies are diversifying, changing, merging, expanding, collaborating, networking and withdrawing from the market place. These actions require continuous refinement, updating, and learning new competencies. These requirements of changing competencies are satisfied by proactive and quick response from HR department. Accordingly, there is a need of adjusting the subsequent core and HR processes of the organization.

HR department can assess the competencies of employees on various aspects of current and future role and design HR interventions keeping in mind the core business of the organization. It may promote self-assessment, peer assessment, and assessment by experts for achieving HR goals of the organization. The human resources management is considered to be a key to manage the core business of the organization and competency framework is the bedrock of HR processes.

2. Concept of Competency

The term 'competency' is not a new term, but it has gained considerable importance in the present day industrial scenario. Competencies remain at the heart of all successful HR processes. The competency is a link between the role and the role holder as shown in Fig. 1.1.

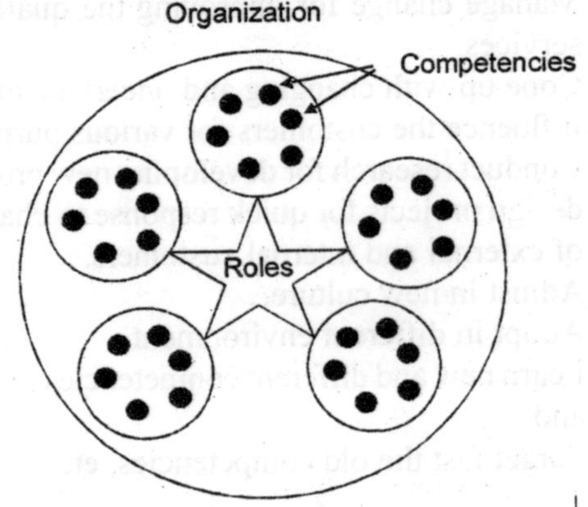

Fig. 1.1 : Organization, Role and Competencies

It enables the role holder to perform competently, proficiently, productively, creatively, and innovatively to assure quality of products and services at minimum price, without waste, on right time, with minimum efforts and without stress.

The term competency is defined by experts in different manner considering the context of the business. It is used synonymously for ability, competence, skills, capabilities, and strengths of employees, etc. The definitions of competency propagated by various experts in different contexts are given below. It is interesting to note that the definition of the 'competency' changes with occupation and time.

- Competencies are ability to perform role in real life situation. [Gupta, 2008]
- Competency is the ability to do or perform or take responsibility. [Race, 2005]
- Competencies are, in essence, definitions of expected performance that, taken as a whole, should provide users with the complete picture of the most valuable behaviours, values and tasks required for their organization's success. [Rankin, 2004]
- Competencies are the behaviours that individuals demonstrate when undertaking job relevant tasks effectively within a given organizational context. [Whiddett & Hollyforde, 2004]
- A competency is an underlying characteristic of a person which enables them to deliver superior performance in a given job, rolc or situation. [Boulter, 2004]
- The competency is a statement which describes the integrated demonstration of a cluster of related knowledge, skills and attitudes that are observable and measurable, necessary to perform a job independently at a prescribed proficiency level. [Earnest, 2001]
- A competency is an underlying characteristic of a person, which enables them to deliver superior performance in a given job, role or situation. [Marshall, 1996]
- The word 'competencies' is used in many contexts, with very different meanings. Basically, competencies fall into three categories or types : Organizational competencies – unique factors that make an organization competitive; Job/role competencies – things an individual must demonstrate to be effective in a job, role, function, task, or duty, an organizational level, or in the entire organization. Personal competencies – aspects of an individual that imply a level of skill, achievement, or output. [Byham, 1996]
- Competence means a skill and standard of performance whilst competency refers to behaviour by which it was achieved. It means that competence describes what people do and competency describes how people do it. [Rowe, 1995]
- Essentially, competencies underlie the behaviours thought

necessary to achieve a desired outcome. A competency is something you can demonstrate. [Weightman, 1994]

- A threshold competency is a person's generic knowledge, motive, trait, self-image, social role or skill, which is essential in performing a job, but is not causally related to superior job performance. [Boyatzis, 1982]
- A job competency is an underlying characteristic of a person in that it may be a motive, a trait, a skill, an aspect of one's self image or social role, or a body of knowledge which he or she uses. A job competency is an underlying characteristic of a person which results in effective and/or superior performance in a job. [Klemp, 1980]
- The concept of competency based instruction is based on the idea that student must be able to demonstrate that they can successfully perform job competencies to the standards accepted by industry. The job "competencies" are the skills, task, knowledge and attitudes that students must learn to perform a job successfully. [Maxwell, 1980]
- A generic knowledge, motive, trait, social role or skill of a person linked to superior performance on the job. [Hayes, 1979]
- Competencies are those tasks, skills, attitudes, values, and appreciations that are deemed critical to successful employment. [Finch & Crunkilton, 1979]
- Competencies are composite skills behaviour or knowledge that can be demonstrated by the learner and are derived outcomes of learning. The emphasis in competency based education is on competencies, on the ability, develop and demonstrate a total performance not just the mere learning on specific skills. [Hall, 1976]
- Competency for a job can be defined as a set of human attributes that enable an employee to meet and exceed expectations of his internal as well as external customers and stakeholders. [Kotwal Milind]

3. Features of Competency

A critical analysis of the above definitions reveals the basic features of competency. These features are stated in Fig. 1.2.

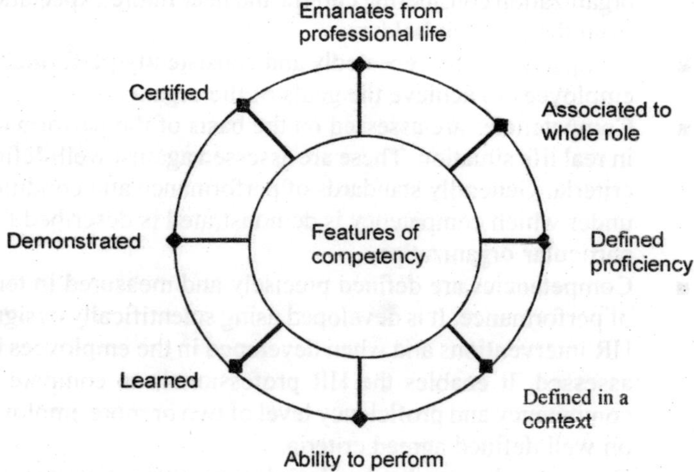

Fig. 1.2 : Features of Competency

- Competencies are derived from the real life professional roles and jobs and it is based on whole work of the employees in the organization. The role of the employees is derived from organizational goals, and current and near future requirements of the plans.
- Competency is a cluster of knowledge, skills, attitudes, and experience which enables employees to perform the role with the available resources in current working environment. So, it is inter-woven with the core business plans and strategy of the organization.
- Competencies and proficiency level in each competency is objectively defined. Proficiency level is related to expected standard of performance and behaviour with reference to core business of the organization.
- Competencies are charted to prepare the *competency framework, competency profile and competency map* which are used for scientific design and implementation of HR processes in the organization.
- The organization provides enough flexibility to employees to learn and develop the competency and proficiency in each competency. The organization also provides autonomy to use the competency for improving the quality of the business.
- Competencies are professionally charted for each role in the

organization considering current and near future expectations from the position holders.

- Competencies are repeatedly and consistently performed by employees to achieve the goals of the organization.
- Competencies are assessed on the basis of the performance in real life situation. These are assessed against well-defined criteria. Generally standards of performance and conditions under which competency is demonstrated is described for a particular organization.
- Competencies are defined precisely and measured in terms of performance. It is developed using scientifically designed HR interventions and when developed in the employees it is assessed. It enables the HR professionals to compare the competency and proficiency level of two or more employees on well defined agreed criteria.
- Competencies can be developed using various strategies at organizational and individual level.

4. Examples of Competencies

The competencies are always written in a particular business environment of the organization. The competencies may be common for organizations in same business. The competencies are stated in active form in which the behavioural outcomes are observable and measurable. Some indicative examples of competency statements are given below :

- Design overhead water tank for domestic water supply scheme.
- Solve the problems related to failure of transformers of distribution line.
- Lead various teams to craft the vision of the organization.
- Prepare a survey report on health condition of children below five years, based on the survey data.
- Make final presentation of project proposal in front of funding agencies to get approval.
- Develop script for recording video lecture.
- Conduct case study session to achieve learning objectives.
- Identify training needs of junior engineers based on training needs survey.

- Prepare a training plan to satisfy identified training needs for developing counseling skills in teachers.
- Prepare power point presentation on project report.

5. Classification of Competencies

The competencies are classified as stated in subsequent paragraphs. The classification of competencies is governed by the nature of the business of the organization. The organizations may use suitable classification criteria for classifying the competencies of the position holders. There could be different classification for different position holders in the same organization. As stated earlier in this chapter that the immediate source for deriving the competencies is the role of the position holder so the role description guides to decide the classification criteria.

Essential Competencies

These are the competencies related to core role of the position holder which contributes to core business of the organization. These are also called compulsory, primary, and core competencies. In different organizations, these competencies are different. For example, the core competencies for a lecturer working in engineering college offering undergraduate programmes are : to prepare instructional plans, implement instructional plans, design learning resources, conduct formative and summative evaluation, organize industrial training of students, etc.

For a person working in customer care department, some of the essential competencies are: establish relationship with customer, appreciate the complaint, take immediate action to remove complaint, remove complaint, inform complainant, prepare profile of complaints, and take preventive action to prevent complaints in future. The essential competencies for a position holder may be desirable for a person working at same level but in different capacity. The essential competencies are used for selection, recruitment, deployment, redeployment, career advancement, identifying training needs, and providing rewards.

Desirable Competencies

These are the competencies related to desirable role of the position holder which contributes to core and peripheral business of the organization. These are also called secondary competencies. For example the desirable competencies for a lecturer working in engineering college offering undergraduate programmes are : to develop curriculum, design continuing education programmes, implement continuing education programmes, organize entrepreneurship development programmes, organize competitions on technical subjects etc. The desirable competencies are used along with essential competencies for taking decision when competitors for a particular position are more and the company wants to select the best.

Optional Competencies

These are the competencies related to role of the position holder which contributes less but need to perform for core and peripheral business of the organization. For example, the optional competencies for a lecturer working in engineering college offering undergraduate programmes are organize cultural, sports and environmental activities of students, recommend books for the library, introduce innovations in the laboratory etc.

Present Competencies

These are the competencies related to role of the position holder which are required to perform core and peripheral business of the organization in present and near future say one year. But suppose the organization is shifting from one technology to other or one customer base to other, or one approach of management to other in such a case competencies required to perform future roles are considered for all HR process. For example, the engineering college is shifting from traditional practices of instruction to multimedia and student centred approaches in such situation the previously mentioned competencies are required to run the current programmes and future competencies such as to develop multimedia packages, manage on line learning, certify the achievement of learning competencies are the future competencies. In fact present competencies act as a base for practicing future competencies.

Peripheral Competencies

These are competencies related to role of the position holder which are required to perform core and peripheral business of the organization not in direct manner but indirectly. For example, the peripheral competencies for customer manager are liaison with internal stakeholders, communicate effectively, know functions of different sections of the organization, etc.

Routine Competencies

These are the competencies that are used by role holders very often to do the day-to-day business of the organization. These are also called traditional competencies. For example, conduct instructional sessions is a routine competency for a lecturer. Receive complaints and console complainant are routine competency for customer care manager.

Non-Routine Competencies

These are the competencies that are used once in a month or over a period of time. These may be essential for a position holder. These competencies are used to implement schemes, projects and programmes which are one time events. For example, prepare a project report to digitize the library is a non-routine competency for lecturer working in electronics, design a laboratory manual is a non-routine competency for a lecturer.

Innovative Competencies

There are many organizations that are always in a continuous change process. They go on improving the products and services according to needs of the society. In such organizations the position holders have to use innovative competencies for improving the products and services and their quality. These are also called entrepreneurial competencies. For example, research and development organization, software industry, banking sector, hospitals are such organizations. The innovative competencies are : evolve strategy, develop technology, increase customer base, expand market share, etc.

Engineering Competencies

These are the competencies related to pure engineering role of the position holder which are required to perform core engineering business of the organization. For example, design of a bridge, design of the transformer, develop a plan of township etc.

Managerial Competencies

These are the competencies that are related to managerial aspect of the role of the individuals or team as a whole. These competencies enable a person to perform the managerial and leadership role dimensions apart from other role dimensions. As the person moves in higher position the managerial and leadership aspects of the role become significant so the role holder is required to acquire the managerial competencies. For example, lead a team to achieve challenging goals, manage inventory to facilitate production, organize resources to manage crisis, negotiate with suppliers, etc.

Change Management Competencies

These are the competencies used in those organizations that are working in dynamic environment. The position holders are expected to design and introduce changes in system, processes, technology etc. at a faster rate. In such a situation these competencies are acquired and used by most of the employees of the organization. For example, in Information Technology, Banking sector, Nano technology related industries and Research organizations these competencies are required in almost all the employees. In some other organizations these competencies are required in some position holders for designing and implementing change as and when required. For example, use of management philosophy, use of new technology, use of recent approaches, conduct survey, evolve strategy etc.

Self-Development Competencies

These are the basic competencies required in all the employees so that they can perform according to changing requirements of the role. These are also related to, adaptation, coping, adjusting, refining, and compromising requirements of the situation. The role holders use these competencies for assessing their needs, potential, strengths and preferences and accordingly set aspirations, ambitions, vision and put efforts to achieve the same.

Threshold Competencies

The characteristics which job holder needs to have to do that job effectively – but do not distinguish the average from superior performer

[Nick Boulter *et al.* 2004]. These competencies are used at entry level for different positions in the organization. These competencies are developed in education and training institutions. These competencies are certified by statutory organizations.

Differentiating Competency

The characteristics which superior performers have but are not present in average performers. [Nick Boulter *et al.*, 2004]. The threshold competencies are used by stakeholders to perform the job at the beginning of the career for a post. Gradually they get experienced and refine their core competencies and proficiency. They get opportunities to develop higher competencies on the job. In many cases professionals develop highest level of competencies and proficiency. They develop unique competencies related to core business of the organization. These competencies provide them competitive leverage to perform differently.

Elemental Competency

It is an ability to do a particular type of task. A job consists of many different types of tasks, thus requiring different elemental competencies. [Kotwal Milind]

Generic Competency

These are the profession related competencies required in each and every employee of the organization. The generic competencies for middle level manager are : planning, leading, decision-making, problem analysis, evaluation, sensitivity, communication, receiving and providing feedback, and self-development and so on.

Meta Competencies

These are the competencies required in employees to learn on their own in changing internal as well as external environment. These competencies may be critical for professionals working in companies expanding on products, services, market and so on. The demand of meta competencies in many companies have created pressure on institutions of higher learning to initiate the development of these competencies so that the professional can use and refine them as and when necessary. Whiddett & Hollyforde, (2004) define these competencies as ability to learn.

Central and Surface Competencies

It may be mentioned that competencies exist at surface as well as at core personality level. The surface level competencies of knowledge and skills are visible in behaviour or performance and can be developed with appropriate training and development. However, the core motives and trait competencies reside deep within and are difficult to understand, measure and develop. [Sharma, 2003]

The classification of competencies depends on the type of the organization. In construction industry working safely may be peripheral or desirable competency but in chemical industry or production industry it can be essential/core competency.

6. Source of Competencies

In competitive world professionally managed organizations have well crafted vision, mission, goals, policies, mandate, and culture of the organization. These sources are used to prepare strategic, perspective, and operational plans of the organization. The plans are implemented by employees of the organization in role sets. The role set is the source of deriving the roles of different position holders in a given context. On the basis of role and role dimensions the competency cluster and competencies are derived, defined, classified and validated. The process of deriving competencies is stated in Fig.1.3.

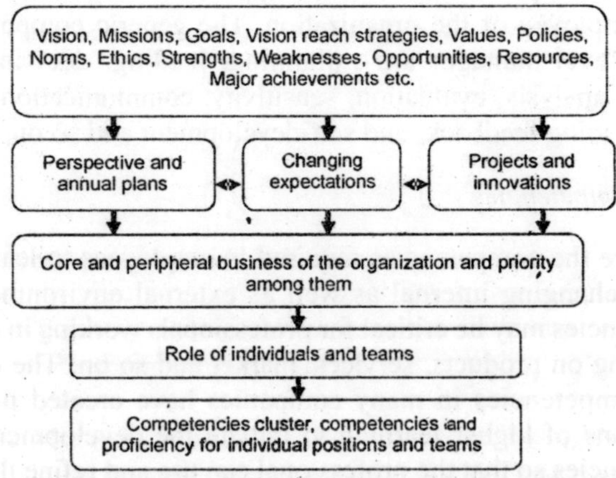

Fig. 1.3: Sources of Deriving Competencies

For example, the role of the director of technical institution is derived and described on dimensions stated in Fig. 1.4. These role dimensions are used to identify the competency cluster and competencies are stated under each cluster. A comprehensive list of competencies under each cluster is given in chapter 3 Format 3.2.

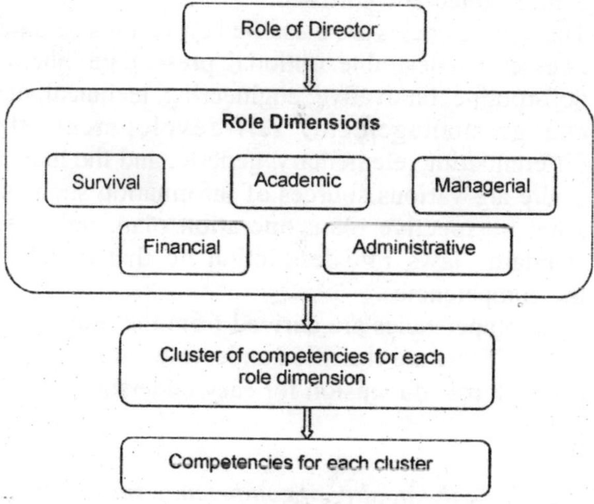

Fig. 1.4 : Role and Competencies

7. Summary

- There is a dire need to perform professionally individually and collectively in changing external and internal environment of the organization.
- There is a need for sustaining, improving and innovating business goals and strategies to achieve them.
- The organizations need to develop employees as professional who can individually and collectively perform professionally in dynamic, uncertain and unfamiliar situations accepting challenges of the business.
- The organizations need to design HR processes and HR interventions for assuring quality, effectiveness, and efficiency in human processes.
- The competency is the unit used to measure, assess, develop and deploy human potential.
- The competency is the cluster of knowledge, skills, attitudes,

and experiences which enable a person to perform role in a given context and situation.

- The competency has features such as it emanates from professional role, associated with the whole role, defines proficiency, defined in a context, ability to perform, learned, demonstrated and certified.
- The competencies are classified on various parameters such as essential, desirable, optional, present, peripheral, routine, non-routine, innovative, engineering, technical, managerial, change management, self-development, threshold, differentiating, elementary, generic, and the like.
- There are various sources of information such as strategic plan, perspective plan, operation plan, policies, culture, standards, laws, role description etc. that are used to derive the competencies.
- The competencies are derived from the role of the position holder. These are classified under role dimensions and cluster for each role dimension for easy understanding.

8. Formats

***Format 1.1:** Check the quality of competency statement*

Check the quality of core competency statements related to any role in your organization against criteria mentioned below :

1. Emanates from professional life.
2. Associated with whole role.
3. Proficiency level defined.
4. Competency is defined in a context.
5. Ability to perform.
6. Competency can be developed.
7. Competency can be demonstrated.
8. Competency can be certified.

Check the Quality of Competency Statement

Sl. No	*Competencies*	*Criteria*							
		1	2	3	4	5	6	7	8

9. Review Questions

1. Define competency in organizational context.
2. Explain the importance of competency in human resources management.
3. State five professional competencies used in your organization.
4. Compare various definitions of competency.
5. Explain the features of competencies.
6. State five competencies possessed by you.
7. Analyze the definitions of competency propagated by various experts and give your definition considering the business of your organization.
8. List the elements of competency.
9. Distinguish between competency and ability.
10. State various parameters for classifying the competencies.
11. Which classification of competencies is suitable for your role? Why?
12. List the sources of information used for listing the competency.

10. Activities for HR Managers

Activity 1.1: List the competencies required to perform your role in the organization.

Activity 1.2: Compare competencies required for your role with other role of same level in your organization.

Activity 1.3: State three competencies which will be required to perform future role.

2

Competency Framework

LEARNING OBJECTIVES

After reading this chapter the readers will be able to :

- Define the concept of competency framework.
- Describe the need and importance of competency framework.
- Explain the use of competency framework.
- Describe the characteristics of competency framework.
- State the factors affecting competency framework.

1. Introduction

Competency framework is a base skeleton for managing the human resources according to the needs of the business. An organization with rich competency framework may facilitate the growth and development of the organization. So the competency framework facilitates the business of the organization and business of the organization guides the refinement of the competency. The organization having well researched competency framework can design effective human resources management (HRM) interventions to satisfy the changing need of the customer and business.

2. Concept of Competency Framework

The competency framework for an organization is a bundle of competencies derived from the vision, missions, goals, vision reach strategies, values, policies, norms, ethics, strengths, weaknesses, opportunities, resources, major achievements, customers and stakeholders' expectations etc. in order to know the nature of human resources required to carry out the business effectively and efficiently. There are number of organizations who are traditionally functioning and have not professionally worked on vision, missions, values etc. If they do not have well crafted vision, missions, plans etc. they should first work on it and then work on competency framework. Otherwise the competency framework will not bring much of improvement and innovations in the performance of the organizations. It is interesting to note that organizations working in similar business may have different framework of competencies because of their unique vision.

3. Need and Importance of Competency Framework

The need and importance of competency framework is stated below:

- *Objectivity :* It provides objectivity in deciding, designing, implementing and evaluating the HRM processes.
- *Tool of Communication :* It is a strong tool of communication for communicating with external and internal stakeholders of the organization on various dimensions of HR processes.
- *Unity of Actions :* It provides unity of actions among various departments, sections, and teams of the organization in HR processes. It also provides unity in actions in organizations working in same trade.
- *Alignment of HR Processes with Vision of the Organization :* The competency framework precisely spells out the roles related competencies that are useful in aligning the HR processes with organizational processes. So HR processes and actions can be appropriately designed and aligned in order to achieve the organizational goals. The redundant actions and activities in HR processes can be dropped to save time, money and energy.
- *Organization of Resources:* Well-designed HR processes help to organize all types of resources at the right time to implement the processes of the organization.
- *Base for Human Resources Development :* The competency based training, education, and learning becomes the base for developing the employees of the organization in order to implement the core processes effectively and efficiently.
- *Plan of the Organization :* The strategic, perspective, and operational plan can be developed professionally using competitive advantages of competency.

- *Marketing Products and Services of the Organization* : The product and services of the organization are professionally developed assuring the quality, fulfilling the national and international requirements to facilitate to market the products and services at higher value.
- *Comparability* : Benchmarking of employees' competency helps in comparability of employees within the organization and with other organizations. It helps to develop required competencies at right time to satisfy business requirements.
- *Universal Acceptability* : Competency is universally acceptable so easy recognition of capability and capacity of employees.
- *Selection Test* : Selection tests to recruit the employees for higher positions, freshers as well as experienced can be designed and used repetitively. It saves time, efforts and money in selection process. Selection of right person for right position is possible.
- *Attracting Professionals* : There are professionals available in the market to excel best in their field of interest. They can be attracted using competency framework approach.
- *Valid and Reliable Certification* : The objectivity in measurement of learning outcomes and level of proficiency in competency is helpful in certification of competency profile and proficiency level.
- *Establishing Equivalence* : The competencies are inherently modular and, therefore, recognized all over the world. So recognition and accreditation of competencies can be given anywhere in the world. Further education can be planned at any time in the professional life of employees as per requirement.
- *Flexibility in Achieving Competencies* : Competencies and cluster of competencies can be grouped to perform a particular role. The competencies/group of competencies can be achieved at any time, duration and place.

4. Use of Competency Framework

The competency framework, competency profiles, and competency map are predominantly and frequently used by HR managers and other significant decision makers for managing HR processes in the organization. As stated in Figs. 1.2 and 1.3, the competency framework should emanate from the professionally designed plans of the organization to take the competitive advantage of it. Similarly the competency profile also supports the professional planning and performance at organizational level. The competency framework, competency development and business development are mutually dependent.

It is useful in ensuring professionalism in all HR processes and thereby ensuring achievement of goals at organizational level. It facilitates best HR practices in the organization. It is useful in enhancing competencies, commitment and culture of the organization for satisfying the internal as well as external customers. It is a system based approach so that continuous improvement in the performance of HR processes is ensured.

It is equally useful for individuals in many ways such as identifying the self-potential, preparing self-development plans, undertaking self-development activities, projecting self on different occasions and building self-image. The use of competency framework is stated in subsequent paragraphs.

Manpower Planning

The competency framework is useful for manpower planning for organizations that are at development phase. It helps to decide what type and how many employees are needed to achieve the organizational goals. It is a good tool for the HR department to decide whether to recruit the employee permanently or temporarily, hire the expertise, redeploy the internal employees, outsource the task etc. The HR department justifies the manpower requirement using competency framework. It helps to optimize the human efforts without compromising with level of satisfaction of individuals and teams. Rather it helps in enhancing productivity at organizational level and joy of performing at individual level.

Recruitment of Employees

The competencies are used for recruiting the right persons for right role in the organization. The person may be from inside or outside the organization. The competencies are used to assess the performance of the candidates with reference to the role to be performed in the organization. The competency framework, profile and map are prepared of a particular position and advertised for recruitment purpose. It is used by potential candidates for self-evaluation purpose. The candidates satisfy themselves about their competence and then apply for the position so that it reduces the efforts required to scrutinize the applications by HR department. It encourages right candidates to apply for the post and discourages rest of the candidates to apply. It is used during scrutiny of the applications of the candidates by HR department. The competencies are used for selecting right candidate for a particular post. It is useful in selecting the best candidates who possesses all essential, desirable and optional competencies and high proficiency in each competency. The right selection of right person for a post requires less training and orientation thereby saves training expenses and provides more time for production. It helps in retaining the person in the organization.

Deployment and Redeployment of Employees

The deployment and redeployment of employees in all types of organizations have become paramount for effective and efficient functioning of the organization and satisfying the psychological, professional, and social needs of the employees. The role related potential of the employees can be diagnosed and they are developed through training, coaching, and mentoring to assume higher positions and challenges of the organization. The competency framework, competency profile and competency map help in appropriately deploy, redeploy, and rotate the employees for different roles in contrast to deployment on the basis of experiences and qualifications. There are a number of positions in the organization where there is no adequate work to be performed for persons in such situation they need to be redeployed for different tasks so that their full time is utilized for productivity. There are roles which are of routine types and require rotation after a certain period of time to keep the person self-motivated. The competency framework is useful to provide them choice for selecting the task and developing themselves for the new task. In such a case they perform multiple roles with interest.

Performance Appraisal

The competency profile developed for a particular position is useful in planning the performance according to competency and proficiency of the person against the competency profile. It is observed that persons working on same position do not possess all the competencies and equal level of proficiencies in each competency. So performance planning based on the strengths of a person on competency profile is promoted and same is used for performance assessment and rewards.

Performance appraisal based on competency profile balances the requirement of the business at the same time distribute the goals and objectives of the organization to different position holders for taping their strengths. In this way the work related stress of the employees may be reduced to a great extent. This approach reduces the training and development cost also.

Training and Development

The competency framework and profile become the base for identifying the training needs at organizational, departmental, team, and individual level. The training needs so identified are used for designing and conducting the training and development programmes effectively and efficiently.

The competency framework and profile are also useful in evaluating the impact of training and development programmes. The guidance, counseling, mentoring activities are also designed and implemented aligned to competency framework of the organization. The employees are aware about their competency profile and other competency profiles so they also take initiatives to develop set of competencies to grab the opportunities available in the organization for their career and professional development.

Succession Planning

It is most neglected dimension of managing human resources in most of the organizations because the organizations use reactive approaches in managing the business as well as human resources. They wake up when employees retire or quit the job. A vacuum is created for some time and somebody takes up the responsibility to perform with the excuses that she/he is not trained, it is not her/his responsibility, it is additional responsibility, and the like.

In the absence of competency framework and competency profile the organization takes up *ad hoc* decisions and the situation gets worse. Competency framework and profile are the strong base to plan and develop people for assuming higher responsibilities immediately whenever situation arises. It is a means for providing career development opportunities to employees through succession planning initiatives.

Retention of Employees

In competitive and global environment ample opportunities are being created everyday for competent and proficient employees. The unsatisfied employees search for such opportunities. In such situations it becomes very difficult to retain the employees. Competency framework and profile are a good means to keep the employees' commitment high for the organization because they can see the career development opportunities, succession plans, compensation and incentives for professional performance and the like. The HR department can identify and negotiate with such employees using competency framework and other development plans of the organization.

Deciding Pay and Incentives

The capability and capacity of the employees are assessed against the competency framework of the organization, competency profile, and role requirement of a particular position. There are some positions which are crucial to performance of the organization that makes the competitive difference in achievement of business goals.

People possessing competencies aligned to such key performance areas are important for the organization. It may be possible that availability of professionals for these crucial areas may be less than demanded within the organization and outside the organization. Same logic is applicable for other positions which are of moderate significance and trivial and employees are available within and outside the organization. In some situations compensation and incentives can be directly linked to the competencies and proficiency possessed by employees. This approach is rational and enhances the satisfaction of employees. This approach helps in retaining superior and critical performers of the organization. It attracts outside professional to join the organization. The relationship between the competencies of employees and compensation and incentives is stated in Fig. 2.1.

5. Assumptions for Developing Competency Framework

The competency framework can be designed and implemented for any organization at any phase of development and it will result in better quality of human processes and performance of the organization

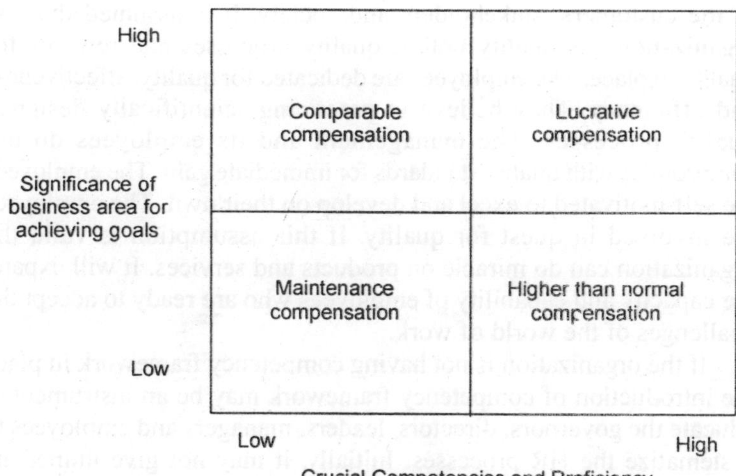

Fig 2.1 : Business Area, Competency of Employees and Compensation

as well as individuals. The competency framework brings best and immediate results in those organizations that fulfil the requirements of assumptions as stated in Fig. 2.2 These assumptions are briefly described in subsequent paragraphs.

Fig. 2.2 : Assumptions for Developing Competency Framework

Commitment for Excellence

The governing body, management of the organization and employees are committed for quality of products and services that satisfies needs of the customers, stakeholders and society. It is assumed that the organization has quality policy, quality processes and rewards for quality in place. The employees are dedicated for quality, effectiveness and efficiency. They believe in practicing scientifically designed quality processes. The management and its employees do not compromise with quality standards for immediate gain. The employees are self-motivated to excel and develop on their own. The employees are involved in quest for quality. If this assumption is valid the organization can do miracle on products and services. It will expand the capacity and capability of employees who are ready to accept the challenges of the world of work.

If the organization is not having competency framework in place the introduction of competency framework may be an instrument to educate the governors, directors, leaders, managers and employees to systematize the HR processes. Initially, it may not give immediate significant results. The fruits of competency framework are varied and many. It all depends on the level of organizational functioning on quality parameters.

Autonomy

Competency framework is beneficial in organizations where the autonomy has percolated down the line. Employees enjoy autonomy to take decisions related to their core processes and roles. The employees are empowered to perform professionally without tension and stress. There is no organizational provision for following a rigid path with compulsion. Now the time has come where the discipline barriers should be removed and total flexibility should be provided to employees to excel better using competency framework.

Competent HR Managers

The managers and employees are competent to provide products and services desired by customers. They are capable to satisfy the changing requirements of the customers and stakeholders. They get an opportunity to work and feel the corporate culture. They are generously sponsored for training in emerging and new areas. At the same time they are trained to assure quality. They are encouraged to conduct researches and experiments to enhance the quality, efficiency and effectiveness of products and services.

Adequate Facilities

The organization has adequate facilities in terms of men, material, machine, money, time and information to perform the activities. The organizational members are having healthy relationship among themselves and with the customers. The organization has network and collaboration with centre of excellences and resource centres. The values and norms of the organization promote motivational culture and climate. The organization provides right kind of inputs at right time for carrying out the activities. The teamwork, creativity, innovation, development and value addition in performance is encouraged and appreciated by one and all.

6. Characteristics of Competency Framework

As stated earlier competency framework is contextual and depends on many factors such as level of professionalism expected in the organization, phase of the organization on development continuum, age group of employees, generation of technology, acceptability of change, availability of resources, opportunities for training and development, opportunities for excelling better, future plans and the like. The generic characteristics of competency framework are stated in Fig. 2.3 and briefly explained.

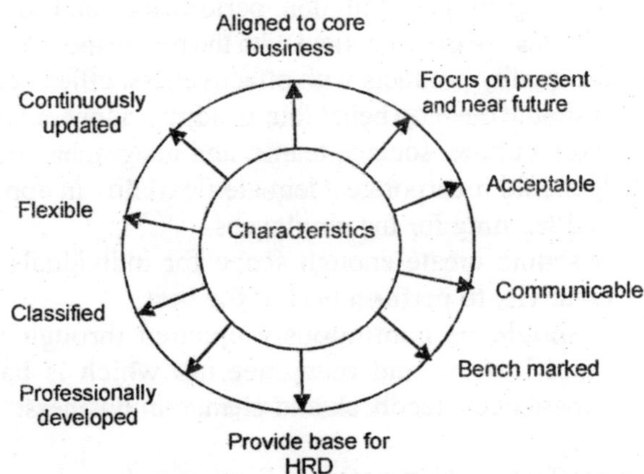

Fig. 2.3 : Characteristics of Competency Framework

- Its main focus should be core business of the organization. Its main focus should be present and near future considering the requirements of the vision of the organization. It should be broad enough to uncover the business of the organization.

- It should be acceptable to governing body, top management, and employees of the organization.
- It should be concrete, specific, clear, self-explanatory, achievable, measurable, communicable, worth for the organization as a whole, and observable. The terms used in defining the competency should be defined.
- It should accelerate HR processes and create individual and collective development opportunities.
- It should classify the competencies such as essential, desirable, optional, routine, non-routine and the like.
- It should be professionally and logically designed using scientific and research methods in contrast to casual approach. It is designed by a team of experts drawn from various disciplines such as technologist, educationist, psychologist and HR experts.
- It should describe the roles that need to be professionally performed by employees. It addresses the need of multiple, variety of, and shifting of roles. It also describes about the positions that can be assumed by employees in different capacities in the organization.
- It should match with different entry behaviour of employees on various aspects such as social, cultural, general intelligence, learning attitude, ambition, performance and so on.
- It should be benchmarked with the best in the world to produce the quality products with effectiveness, efficiency and ease.
- It should develop behaviour to adjust, adopt, adapt in diverse work culture, society, teams, and geographic areas.
- It should incorporate adequate flexibility in approach, time, and learning for the employees.
- It should create enough scope for individuals and teams' creativity to perform best of the best.
- It should be continuously updated through refinement, modification, and reengineering which is based on the experiences, feedback and change in business.

7. Factors affecting Competency Framework

The effectiveness and efficiency of competency framework approach in any organization is affected by numerous factors. These factors are classified as facilitating factors and restraining factors. If the magnitude and intensity of facilitating factors are more than the magnitude and intensity of restraining factors the task of developing and using competency framework becomes easy for the team and organization. Otherwise it will find place in documents of the organization. The team sincerely works to channelize the facilitating factors during the process of competency framework development. At the same time it designs and uses strategies to minimize the effect of restraining factors. The general facilitating and restraining factors are stated in Fig. 2.4.

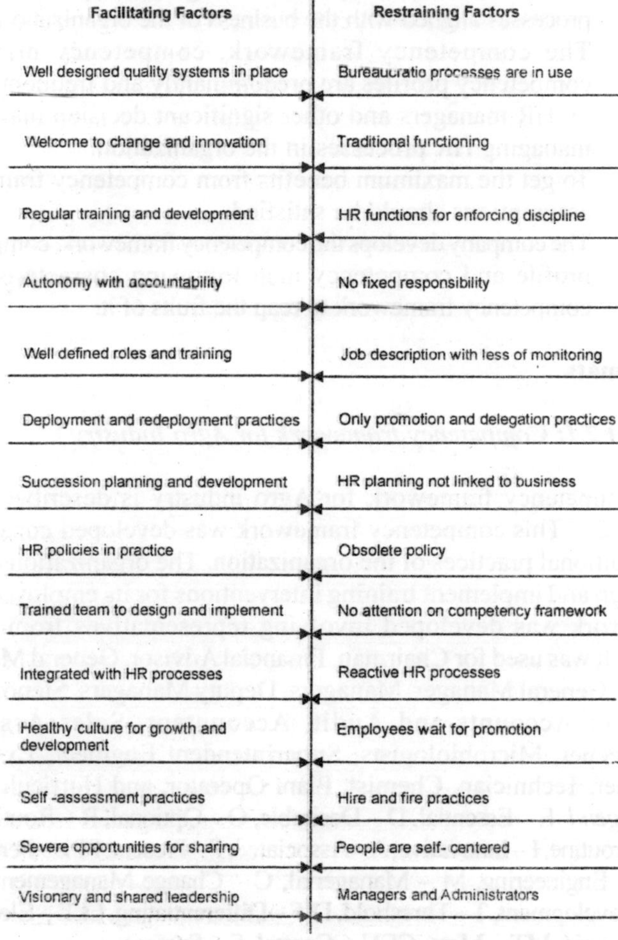

Fig. 2.4 : Factors Affecting Competency Framework

8. Summary

- The competency framework for an organization is a bundle of competencies derived from the vision, missions, goals, vision reach strategies, values, policies, norms, ethics, strengths, weaknesses, opportunities, resources, major achievements etc. in order to know the nature of human resources required to carry out the business effectively and efficiently.
- The organization prepares competency framework, competency profile and competency map to design and implement human processes aligned with the business of the organization.
- The competency framework, competency map, and competency profiles are predominantly and frequently used by HR managers and other significant decision makers for managing HR processes in the organization.
- To get the maximum benefits from competency framework assumptions should be satisfied.
- The company develops the competency framework, competency profile and competency map following characteristics of competency framework to reap the fruits of it.

9. Formats

Format 2.1: Competency framework for Agro Industry

The competency framework for Agro industry is described in the format 2.1. This competency framework was developed considering the traditional practices of the organization. The organization wanted to design and implement training interventions for its employees. The framework was developed involving representatives from all the cadres. It was used for Chairman, Financial Advisor, General Manager, Deputy General Manager, Managers, Deputy Managers, Steno, Clerk, Manager Accounts and Audit, Accountant, Sales Assistant, Storekeeper, Microbiologists, Superintendent Engineer, Executive Engineer, Technician, Chemist, Plant Operator, and Horticulturists.

Legend: E – Essential, D – Desirable, O – Optional, R – Routine, NR – Non-routine, I – Innovative, A – Associated, P – Present, PPL – Peripheral, ENG – Engineering, M – Managerial, C – Change Management, SD – Staff Development, T – Threshold, DIF – Differentiating, ELE – Elemental, G – Generic, MT – Meta, CEN – Central, S – Surface

Competency Framework for Agro Industry

Sl. No.	*Competency framework*	*Type*
1.	Identify key stakeholders.	NR
2.	Develop collaborative linkages with all significant stakeholders	NR
3.	Contribute to clarification of organizational purpose, functions of various units, and derivation of roles of different functionaries	E
4.	Identify and resolve problems	R
5.	Make effective decisions	R
6.	Depict appropriate leadership behaviour in different situations	E, R
7.	Manage conflicts	NR, M
8.	Manage crisis	NR, M
9.	Develop strategies for accomplishing targets and focusing on services with high returns	NR, M
10.	Formulate project and annual work plans using Logical Framework analysis	E, NR, M
11.	Organize for implementing project and annual work plan using appropriate manpower deployment approaches	E, M, R
12.	Develop a marketing and service network involving organizational units and allied agencies	E, M, R
13.	Conduct market research and develop marketing strategies for ensuring and enhancement in market share	R, E, M, R
14.	Evolve project	E, M
15.	Plan project implementation approaches	E, NR
16.	Work in teams	E, NR
17.	Become responsive to client requirements and develop a high sense of client orientation	E, CEN, R
18.	Analyze cost effectiveness of various units and suggest improvement strategies	E, NR
19.	Develop support policy to enable effective performance of various units	M, E
20.	Determine product and services price on the basis of related parameters	R, E, M
21.	Collect performance data and evolve management information system for district, regional units, and headquarters	R, E
22.	Conduct performance and financial audit	E, NR
23.	Use modern methods of accounting	R, E

(Contd.)

Format 2.1: (Contd.)

Sl. No.	Competency framework	Type
24.	Forecast the demands	NR, C, E
25.	Coordinate transportation and assignment process	E, R
26.	Manage inventory using modern methods of inventory management	E, R

10. Review Questions

1. Define competency framework.
2. State the need and importance of having a competency framework for an organization.
3. Explain the use of competency framework for managing HR processes.
4. Describe the characteristics of competency framework.
5. State the factors affecting competency framework.

11. Activities for HR Managers

Activity 2.1: Study the competency framework of your organization and refine it.

Activity 2.2: Identify the factors affecting competency framework of your organization.

3

Competency Framework Development

LEARNING OBJECTIVES

After reading this chapter the readers will be able to :

- Explain the models of competency framework.
- Describe the process of developing competency framework.
- Explain the meaning of competency mapping.
- Describe the guidelines for developing the competency framework.
- Evaluate the competency framework of an organization.

1. Introduction

The models theoretical as well as practical are useful to develop competency framework for the organization. There could be three situations for organizations. The organization may not have any type of competency framework. It may be a traditional organization and practicing traditional HR processes. For such organization a research method is required to be used for developing the competency framework. If this type of organization is functioning on old management processes it should first shift to new one and simultaneously work on the competency framework.

The second type of organization may have developed competency framework long back say five years ago and after that it has expanded business, diversified in products and services, and implemented innovations. But it has not refined and modified the competency framework. For such organization research approach is not required. It can undertake exercises of refining and modifying the competency framework considering the present and future requirements of the organization. The third type of organization may have latest competency framework but still struggling for appropriately using it for HRM. In this chapter an approach to competency framework development is described.

2. Models of Competency

Iceberg Model

Nick Boulter *et.al.* (2004) have proposed this model for managerial competencies. They have stated that competency is an underlying characteristic of a person which enables them to deliver superior performance in a given job, role or situation. They have stated that managerial competencies are like iceberg, with skills and knowledge forming the tip. They stated that underlying elements of competencies are less visible but largely direct and control surface behaviour. Social role and self-image exist at a conscious level, traits and motives exist further below the surface, lying closer to person's core.

People Capability Maturity Model

The scientifically developed competency framework for organization and competency profile for various positions are useful to identify the potential of employees to develop as per developing needs of the organization. So HR development interventions are in tune with their potential. These interventions are systematically designed and implemented in the organization for harnessing the full potential of employees. This approach enhances effectiveness and efficiency at organizational level at the same time it increases satisfaction level of the employees.

The capacity of the employees is harnessed designing various interventions such as deployment, redeployment, delegation of authority, assigning challenging projects, promotions and the like. The business development, HR development and deployment are implemented in integrated manner to create win-win situation for the organization and employees. It provides the base for creating spiral effect in business development.

This model is used in organizations that are in a dynamic business and need to update, improve and innovate business goals and strategies on regular basis. This model creates an opportunity for experimentation, learning, and enhancing the professionalism in business. At the same time it sustains business excellence. The model promotes to create successive sound base for continuous improvement, continual improvement and value addition in business and professionalism. The model is useful in removing and preventing

inefficiency, redundancy, inconsistency in HR processes and thereby in business. At the same time it creates scope for enhancing maturity, capability and capacity of employees to accept the new challenges and develop accordingly. The various phases of enhancing the capability and capacity of professionals using competency framework approach in any organization are shown in Fig. 3.1.

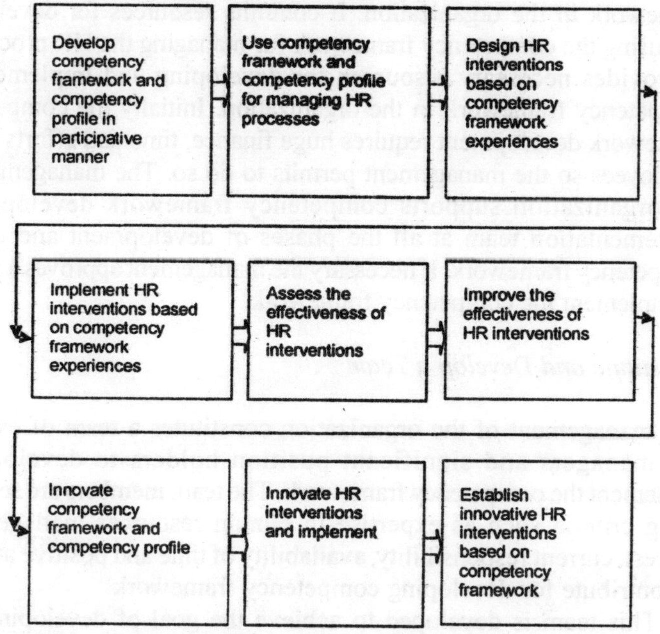

Fig. 3.1 : Phases of Maturity Development

3. Competency Framework Development

The process of development of competency framework at organizational level is an excellent organizational diagnosis approach to identify the strengths and weaknesses of the organization on competency parameters.

The competency framework for the whole organization is developed using a research approach so that the HR processes can be designed to support the core business of the organization. The competency framework is first developed for the organization then for the departments, divisions, sections, teams, and individual positions. The author has used the following model for developing the competency framework for different organizations.

Decision to Develop Competency Framework

The governing body or the society or the empowered decision making body takes the decision to develop and implement the competency framework in the organization. It commits resources for developing and using the competency framework for managing the HR processes. It provides necessary resources for developing and implementing competency framework in the organization. Initially the competency framework development requires huge finance, time and efforts of the employees so the management permits to do so. The management of the organization supports competency framework development, implementation team at all the phases of development and use of competency framework. If necessary the management approves a policy to implement the competency framework.

Constitute and Develop a Team

The management of the organization constitutes a team of experts, HR managers and significant position holders to develop and implement the competency framework. The team members are selected using criteria such as expertise in human resources management, interest, current responsibility, availability of time and positive attitude to contribute for developing competency framework.

This team is developed to achieve the goal of developing and implementing competency framework in the organization. It functions under the leadership of HR department of the organization and facilitated by competency experts. The competency experts and HR experts impart intensive training to the team on topics such as concept, elements, characteristics, classification, benefits and use of competency framework. The team is also trained on models, tools and techniques of developing and using competency framework for competitive advantage.

Prepare Action Plan to Develop and Use Competency Framework

The core team prepares action plan to develop the competency framework for the organization. It includes following activities in preparing action plan :

- Developing learning resources such as concept paper, brochure, handouts, posters, guideline document, frequently asked questions, video film, and power point presentations on various aspects of competency framework.
- Organizing meetings, workshops, focus group discussions, creativity sessions, seminars, etc. with various purposes such as creating awareness on developing and using competency framework, developing and validating competencies for different position holders, defining proficiency level, deciding the criteria for assessment and designing HR interventions.
- Designing and validating instruments for data collection to develop competency framework, competency profile, proficiency and HR interventions.
- Analyzing data for preparing competency framework, competency profile, proficiency, and assessment criteria.
- Preparing and announcing competency framework for comments, validation, and acceptance.
- Implementing competency framework for various purposes as stated in the guideline document or manual.
- Reviewing HR processes in the light of competency framework, competency profile and proficiency.
- Refining, revising, improving, and innovating HR processes through professionally designed HR interventions.
- Monitoring the implementation and use of competency framework and solving day-to-day problems.
- Documenting and reporting the progress of implementation of competency framework and experiences gained in the form of anecdotes and case studies.
- Evaluating the overall performance of the competency framework project and take significant decisions for next cycle.
- Assessing the impact of competency framework project and celebrating the success.

Process of Developing Competency Framework

The team follows the process stated in following paragraphs for developing the competency framework :

(i) *Review the Governance and Management of the Organization*

The team studies the vision, missions, goals, vision reach strategies, values, policies, norms, ethics, strengths, weaknesses, opportunities, resources, major achievements, strategic plan, perspective plan, operational plan, projects, core areas of performance, statutory requirements, present as well as future expected roles and responsibilities of departments, divisions, sections, teams and individuals, expectations of internal as well as external stakeholders, personal aspirations and ambitions of individuals and teams, results of performance appraisal, attrition rate, internal as well as external feedback, business trends, level of competition etc. Team reviews the literature, observes the processes, and gathers preliminary information from sample population. The organizations use diagnosis tools and techniques for this purpose.

The team analyses the current role, job, tasks, activities, responsibility, accountability, duty, incentive and punishment system, culture, authority, method of delegation, criteria for performance assessment, attitudes and ambitions of employees, level of professionalism, grievances, performance problems, role allocation, recruitment process, and so on. The outcomes of study and analysis are useful to list, classify and draw profile of competencies for individual roles.

It is interesting to note that during the review process the team may come across many strengths and weaknesses, opportunities and threats related to various systems of the organization. This output is used for improving the performance of the system. The analysis results may be related to wastage, redundant activities, obsolete technology, incapable employees and so on.

(ii) *Evolve Competencies*

Considering results of review exercise on above parameters, the competencies are listed at organizational level. The competencies may be stated priority-wise or in hierarchical order or in a particular classification. The first draft of the competency framework is prepared and reviewed by a team. The team removes the duplications, overlaps, gaps, and framing problems. All the competencies are stated in the same manner for easy understanding and use. If the organization is large and the list of competencies is too long, it is suggested to encompass the competencies in competency clusters. At this stage the research team may think on classifying the competencies using appropriate classification system. The competencies are stated in specific, observable and measurable terms.

(iii) *Validate and Finalize Competencies at Organizational Level*

The competency framework so developed for the organization is circulated to all the internal and external stakeholders for their comments, observation, suggestion, criticism, and reaction. Their reactions are considered for refining the competency framework at organizational level. The team works on the suggestions received in positive spirit and refines the competency framework. After refining the competency framework it is circulated to selected persons, especially to those who had made critical comments or suggested innovative ideas. After getting the final comments from selected persons it is finalized. The concept of benchmarking is used for enhancing the level and proficiency of the competency and creating challenge in the process of performance. The competency framework development model is shown in Fig. 3.2.

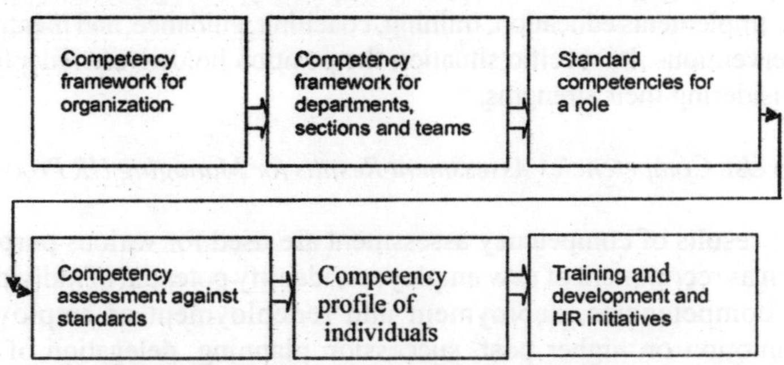

Fig. 3.2 : Competency Framework Development

(iv) *Derive Competencies for Department, Division, Section, Teams, and Positions*

Once the competency framework is evolved it becomes the bedrock for deriving the competency framework for departments, divisions, sections, teams, and individual positions. At this level there could be detailed listing of competencies at micro level. At this level priority, urgency, and requirement can be decided at individual level considering the priority. The competencies listed as peripheral at organizational level may be core for a particular role holder because that person is responsible to perform a particular role. Similarly, the competency listed as core at organizational level may be optional for a particular position holder considering the requirements of the role. Once the competency framework and profile is derived it is circulated to one and all related persons for their comments and suggestions. It is further refined and finalized based on the comments of related persons for designing HR interventions with specific purposes.

(v) *Assess Competencies*

The competency profile for individuals can be drawn against the standard competency of the role. The assessment of competency starts with self appraisal, analysis, and report. Then the superiors, subordinates, peers, and experts are requested to do the appraisal and identify the strengths and weaknesses with respect to standard competency profile. The strengths of individuals are used to deploy and redeploy them for specific purpose. If gaps are found in their competency the organization designs and implements education, training, coaching, guidance, and mentoring interventions. In specific situation the position holders are redeployed considering their strengths.

(vi) *Use Competencies Assessment Results for Managing HR Processes*

The results of competency assessment are used for various purposes such as recruitment of new employees, identify potential of individuals on competencies, deployment and redeployment of employees, promotion on higher post, succession planning, delegation of task and authority, appointment of consultants, education, training and development of employees, decide compensatory package, harness the collective strengths of the employees for competitive advantage, design strategies to cover up the competency gap, etc.

(vii) *Evaluate Impact of Using Competency Framework*

The team evaluates the impact of competency framework on various parameters of functioning of the organization, quality of products and services, and expansion of business. Generally, the impact of competency framework is assessed quantitatively as well as qualitatively on parameters such as product quality, process, features, usability, attractiveness, durability, performance, power consumption, packaging, user manual, technology, etc.

The impact is also assessed on service parameters such as promptness, preventive maintenance, satisfaction of query, cost of production, care in production, reduction in wastage etc. The impact is also measured on behaviour parameters such as polite, stable, helping, attentive, sincere, guiding, sharing, caring, and so on.

The impact is also measured on parameters such as satisfaction level of employees, turn over of employees, deployment and redeployment of employees, attracting eminent persons to get associated with the organization etc. These parameters are decided by organization considering its nature of business and objectives of using competency framework approach.

The advantage of using whole to part model as described is that the performance of whole organization can be improved and innovated managing competency framework at organizational level. The impact of the competency based approach can be seen by one and all within and outside of the organization. On one hand this approach is a proactive approach to improve the performance of the organization and on other hand it enhances the satisfaction level of employees. On the contrary the part to whole approach is not appreciated by other people who are not involved in the process. Its impact is trivial and invisible.

4. Experiences of Competency Framework Development

The author has gained following experiences working with government, public, and private organizations on competency framework development and its use for designing and implementing HRM interventions:

- The author has come across organizations that are functioning traditionally without having vision, missions, quality systems but adopted competency framework system. They have developed competency framework and using it for one or two purposes. It is interesting to note that it is not helping them to come out of their problems. Rather it has created equal number of problems for them. Now they are criticizing the competency framework approach.

- The author has seen that organizations in similar business having different vision, development phase, geographic location etc., have adopted the competency framework of other similar organizations without going in details of the same, are facing numerous problems such as excessive training cost, resistance of employees to develop new and different competencies, non-acceptance of competency framework, questioning the relevance of competency framework, and so on.
- The author has seen that organizations have developed competency framework employing a consultant. The consultant developed the competency framework considering idealistic situation without involving the employees of the organization. Even HR department is not prepared to design the HR strategies based on the competency framework. So the competency framework has become document to show to visitors and dignitaries.
- The author has seen that the organizations have crafted their vision, missions, goals and still working with traditional HR processes. They have not worked out the HR processes based on competency framework so in spite of having state-of-the art resources, latest technology and sound financial conditions they are unable to satisfy the expectations of the customers and stakeholders.
- The author has seen that organization started to develop competency framework but they shifted the focus and efforts to reengineer the functioning of the organization. They planned and implemented many major change simultaneously. Now they are not sure whether to develop the competency framework for changing role or wait till the changes are established.
- The resource persons are weak in stating the competency framework. Because of non-clarity of business and narrow focus of the team members and other HR managers, competencies are confused with role, task, activity, knowledge, skills and experience.
- The competency framework is not updated with different phases of change in the organization. The company adopted the technology and production processes but the full potential is not harnessed in absence of updated competency framework and HR interventions.

- The organizations do not follow the principles of introducing the change in introducing the competency framework so they face a lot of resistance from all the corners.

5. Competency Profile

It is a set of all types of competencies required to perform a particular role in an organization effectively and efficiently in present and near future which contributes significantly for achieving objectives related to core business of the organization. The competency profile for a role of particular position is useful for selection, deployment, redeployment, training and development. As indicated in Fig. 3.2 the competency framework for individuals is developed after deriving the roles and responsibilities at individual position level. The competency profile for education manager is stated in Format 3.2. This set of standard competencies was used to draw the competency profile at national level and indentify the training needs of individuals.

6. Competency Map

Competency mapping is another scientific method for competency analysis. It is a 'spray diagram' or a graphic representation of different types of skills, which constitute a competency. The competency map is generally represented by circles/ellipses enclosing these components and linkage lines indicating their inter-dependence and sequence. From the competency in the middle of the page, pointers branch out in all directions to the different types of skills, facts, rules, and concepts. The competency maps also bring out the attitudes/social skills, interests, etc. which are part of the competency and are, therefore, required to be developed in employees during education, training, coaching and mentoring. The more the number of linkages to an ellipse is an indicator of its greater importance and necessity and hence considered essential for the employees. It should be noted that each skill (cognitive, practical, and social skill) begin with an active verb, whereas facts, concepts, rules, principles may not start with verbs. The competency mapping derivation also requires creativity and analytical thinking. Once the competency map is evolved, practical skills, cognitive skills, social skills and attitudes emerge out without much effort. Competency map is used for education, training, mentoring, coaching and counseling.

7. Guidelines for Developing the Competency Framework

The competency framework development is an important HR process for any organization. It is a participative process so it brings variety of improvements and removes confusions and gaps in HR processes. The guidelines stated below are observed during the process of development of competency framework:

- Study the business, functioning of the organization, resources, culture etc. before going for developing competency framework. If required systematize the major activities and processes before going for competency framework development.
- Organize sufficient awareness and education programmes on competency framework development and remove doubts of employees related to it. In these programmes make the purpose of undertaking competency development research clear to prevent rumour. Give it sufficient publicity and seek participation of one and all.
- Use holistic approach for developing competency framework for the whole organization and for all the positions in contrast to limited purpose and limited positions. Make it a base for all HR interventions.
- Prepare competency framework which works as a skeleton for deriving competencies for all the positions. Refer it when any major change is introduced and refine it in the light of change.
- Write the competency statement following the characteristics of competency statement. If necessary define the domain of competencies at organization level. The common domains are production, maintenance, marketing, customer care, research, logistics, quality assurance, human resources management, projects, finance, networking with organizations, purchase, inventory management, etc.
- If the organization is large and positions are many code the competencies to refer it and avoid any confusion.
- Update the framework according to change in business, focus, and philosophy of functioning. There should not be any gap in core competencies at organization level otherwise it will directly affect the business of the organization.

- Use the principle of necessary and sufficient for developing the competency framework and competency profile. If necessary, show the relative importance or priority of competency in competency framework to fix priority for HR interventions.
- Prepare the competency framework without considering the employees and their level of performance because it is situational. These situations change frequently as the person retires or promoted or shifted.

8. Summary

- The competency framework for an organization is a bundle of competencies derived from the vision, missions, goals, vision reach strategies, values, policies, norms, ethics, strengths, weaknesses, opportunities, resources, major achievements etc. in order to know the nature of human resources required to carry out the business effectively and efficiently.
- The organization prepares competency framework, competency profile and competency map to design and implement human processes aligned with the business of the organization.
- The competency framework, competency map, and competency profiles are predominantly and frequently used by HR managers and other significant decision makers for managing HR processes in the organization.
- The company develops the competency framework, competency profile and competency map following characteristics of competency framework to reap the fruits of it.
- There are number of models of competency framework development out of which iceberg and people capability maturity models are popular. The author suggests research approach to develop competency framework and competency profile.
- The author suggests steps such as decision to develop competency, team formation and development, preparation of action plan, decide process of developing competency, develop competency framework, assess competencies, design

HR interventions, evaluate impact of competency framework and HR interventions.

9. Formats

***Format 3.1**: Audit the Competency Framework of Your Organization*

Instructions for Auditors : Audit the competency framework, its implementation and improvement on the criteria stated in the Format given below. During the audit of competency framework, if you come across deficiencies/gaps/weaknesses, note down the extent of gap in column 3 and description of the gap in column 4 of the format. After auditing the competency framework against each criteria and noting down the deficiencies/gaps/weaknesses think about the improvements in competency framework in the light of various criteria and note it down in column 5. You can think about value additions with respect to the criteria under consideration even if you do not find any weakness and mention it in column 5. Please use following scale for indicating extent of deficiencies/gaps/weaknesses in column 3.

Legend: Deficiency/gap/weakness: 5 – Very high, 4 – High, 3 – Medium, 2 – Low, 1 – Very low, 0 – Nil

Audit the Competency Framework, its Implementation and Improvement

Sl. No.	*Criteria*	*Extent of Gaps*	*Description of Gaps or scope for improvement*	*Strategies to bring improvement*
1	*2*	*3*	*4*	*5*
A.	**Evolve competency framework**			
1.	**Does it serve following purposes at organization level :**			
	• **Growth and development of organization**			
	• **Effective planning of performance of individuals and teams**			
	• **Benchmarking of competencies and performance**			
	• **Human resources development**			

Format 3.1 : *(Contd.)*

Sl. No.	*Criteria*	*Extent of Gaps*	*Description of Gaps or scope for improvement*	*Strategies to bring improvement*
1	*2*	*3*	*4*	*5*
	• Effective deployment and redeployment of human resources • Documentation of performance • Decisions on rewards and incentives • Identifying training and development needs and preparing employee development plans • Succession planning • Performance appraisal			
2.	Does it serve following purposes at individual level : • Exploring potential of individuals • Self-development • Empowering individuals • Creating healthy relationship • Opportunities for learning through feedback, guidance, counseling and mentoring • Self-satisfaction			
3.	Does it satisfy following characteristics : • Communicate the purpose • Indicates prioritization among competencies • Promotes performance planning • Based on data, facts, and figures • Role, job and task oriented • Development oriented • Emphasize on self development • Appraisal of competency by self and all other significant stakeholders • Scientific use of production methods • Acceptable to all the members			

Format 3.1 : (Contd.)

Sl. No.	Criteria	Extent of Gaps	Description of Gaps or scope for improvement	Strategies to bring improvement
1	2	3	4	5
	• Continually updated • Less paper work			
4.	Does it focus on following : • Creativity and innovation • Change and development • Collaborative learning • Performance problem prevention • Rewards, growth, and development • Autonomy with accountability • Effective communication • Career development • Improvement in present as well as future performance			
5.	Is the description of competency : • Comprehensive but precise • Relevant to core and peripheral business • Promote effective planning of HRs • Focus on quantitative as well qualitative performance • Measures end results as well as process effectiveness • Facilitate monitoring and review of the performance • Benchmark performance • Linked to rewards, incentives, and development			
6.	Competency framework based on following points : • Vision, missions, goals, values, plans, norms, ethics, • Key areas of functioning • Roles, responsibility, authority and accountability of different position holders • Criteria for interpretation of proficiency • Appreciation, rewards and			

***Format 3.1 :** (Contd.)*

Sl. No.	*Criteria*	*Extent of Gaps*	*Description of Gaps or scope for improvement*	*Strategies to bring improvement*
1	*2*	*3*	*4*	*5*
	incentives for excellent performance			
B.	**Competency framework implementation**			
7.	Awareness and education of institutional members on competency framework, its use and impact			
8.	Competency awareness and validation workshops conducted and competency framework validated by related position holders			
9.	Commitment of the management to use competency framework for HR and other processes			
10.	Training and development opportunities are created for employees to achieve excellence			
11.	Support, help and guidance provided during competency performance			
12.	Formative appraisal is conducted by self and related persons informally, and constructive feedback is offered for improvement of competency			
13.	Competency framework is reviewed			
C.	**Competency framework improvement**			
14.	Collective learning on competency framework using variety of approaches such as meetings, workshops, interaction sessions, creativity sessions, case studies of critical competencies, Inputs to next year HR planning			
15.	Guidance, counseling, coaching and mentoring for improvement in competencies			

Format 3.1 : (Contd.)

Sl. No.	*Criteria*	*Extent of Gaps*	*Description of Gaps or scope for improvement*	*Strategies to bring improvement*
1	*2*	*3*	*4*	*5*
16.	Training and development opportunities such as action learning, role play, problem based learning, conferences, seminars, panel discussions, quality circles, self learning etc.			
17.	Identifying and removing the gaps in competency framework			
18.	Refinement of performance appraisal system			

***Format 3.2:** Competency Profile of Technical Education Managers*

Name of the respondent :
Designation :
Address :
E-mail :

Kindly rate the competencies (which are not in priority order) given below required for technical education managers (e.g. Directors, Principals, Deans and HODs) by writing 3, 2, 1 or 0 in both columns ('possessed by you' and 'required by you') against each competency (which will be confidential).

Legend: 3 – Great extent, 2— Medium extent, 1—Low extent, 0 —Not required.

Competency Profile

Sl. No.	*Competency Profile of Technical Education Manager*	*Extent of competency*	
		Possessed by you	*Required by you*
A.	**SURVIVAL COMPETENCIES**		
1.	Use information and communication technology (ICT) effectively for institutional development		
2.	Utilize management information system for taking significant decisions		
3.	Undertake self learning to keep abreast with the developments in technical education		
4.	Work effectively with computers		
5.	Handle one's emotions wisely		

Format 3.2 : (*Contd.*)

Sl. No.	*Competency Profile of Technical Education Manager*	*Extent of competency*	
		Possessed by you	*Required by you*
6.	Work with limited resources		
7.	Provide training effectively		
8.	Market institutional services		
9.	Negotiate with specific purposes so as to resolve conflict, enter agreement, manage crisis etc.		
	Any other?		
B.	**ACADEMIC**		
B1	**Planning Competencies**		
10.	Craft shared vision of the institution democratically along with its shared values, ethics and norms		
11.	Market the vision and corporate reputation of the institution		
12.	Develop academic strategic and operation plans of the institution		
13.	Take participative decisions to achieve Specific, Measurable, Achievable Realistic and Time bound goals		
14.	Design education programmes in emerging technologies		
15.	Design continuing education programmes in emerging technologies along with monitoring and feedback mechanisms		
16.	Design need-based training programmes for faculty, industry and society		
17.	Design quality assurance mechanisms		
	Any other?		
B2.	**Implementation Competencies**		
18.	Offer education programmes in emerging technologies		
19.	Conduct continuing educational programmes in emerging technologies		
20.	Conduct need-based training programmes for faculty, industry and society		
21.	Use management tools and techniques for achieving academic excellence		
22.	Implement student support services such as guidance and counseling, entrepreneurship development, training and placement, chapters of professional bodies, etc.		
23.	Conduct researches to improve academic processes		

Format 3.2 : (Contd.)

Sl. No.	Competency Profile of Technical Education Manager	Extent of competency	
		Possessed by you	Required by you
24.	Develop print and non-print learning resources in collaboration with industry for contemporary and emerging technologies		
25.	Evaluate all academic processes against designed plans		
26.	Ensure quality in implementation of institutional plans		
	Any other ?		
B3.	**Liaisoning Competencies**		
27.	Establish linkages with industry for academic improvement		
28.	Undertake joint projects with industries for mutual benefit		
29.	Network with research and resource institutions		
30.	Establish rapport with faculty, staff and students		
	Any other ?		
B4.	**Leadership Competencies**		
31.	Lead teams to undertake research studies		
32.	Lead change/innovation implementation teams effectively		
33.	Lead teams to achieve the SMART goals		
34.	Organize focused meetings, interactions, discussions, workshops, creativity sessions, etc.		
35.	Delegate powers for smooth functioning of the institution		
36.	Develop education leaders		
37.	Coordinate the internal and external activities		
	Any other ?		
B5.	**Academic Culture Building Competencies**		
38.	Adhere to declared values, ethics and norms		
39.	Assess the performance related to values, ethics and norms		
40.	Create opportunities for students and staff to joyfully self learn		
41.	Empower women and girl students for successful careers		
42.	Generate opportunities for the physically challenged students		

Format 3.2 **:** *(Contd.)*

Sl. No.	*Competency Profile of Technical Education Manager*	*Extent of competency*	
		Possessed by you	*Required by you*
43.	Create opportunities for physical, technical, managerial, professional, entrepreneurial, social and spiritual development of the students		
	Any other ?		
C.	**MANAGERIAL**		
C1.	**Policy Support Competencies**		
44.	Design policies for smooth functioning of the institution		
45.	Provide policy support in all the areas of institution functioning such as recruitment, human resources development, rewards, consultancy, students' services, punishment, decentralization of authority and the like		
	Any other?		
C2.	**Human Resources Competencies**		
46.	Recruit right faculty and supporting staff		
47.	Train/retrain the faculty and staff to fulfil the vision of the institution		
48.	Deploy/redeploy the faculty and staff members for successful implementation of academic plans		
49.	Ensure sharing of experiences for institutional development		
50.	Guide and counsel staff and students with constructive feedback		
	Any other?		
C3.	**Resources Managing Competencies**		
51.	Manage physical resources for implementation of designed plans effectively and proactively		
52.	Minimize wastage of resources in functioning of the institution		
53.	Manage infrastructure for achieving academic excellence		
54.	Generate resources		
	Any other?		
C4.	**Marketing Competencies**		
55.	Market the products and services of the institution		
56.	Market institutional strengths to industry		
57.	Survey market to explore opportunities for business		

Format 3.2 : (*Contd.*)

Sl. No.	*Competency Profile of Technical Education Manager*	*Extent of competency*	
		Possessed by you	*Required by you*
	Any other ?		
C5.	**Change and Innovation Competencies**		
58.	Implement innovative curricular and co-curricular changes scientifically for academic excellence		
59.	Seek participation of stakeholders in change management		
60.	Conduct various research studies like curriculum needs analysis, technology prediction study, action research, impact study, tracer study, etc.		
61.	Use innovative curriculum approaches such as competency based curriculum, problem based learning, etc.		
62.	Ensure use of interactive learning resources such as computer aided instruction, multi-media, self-learning, etc.		
63.	Promote industry oriented project-based learning		
64.	Manage production centre competitively		
	Any other ?		
C5.	**Networking Competencies**		
65.	Network with sister institutions, research and resource organizations and centre of excellence		
66.	Collaborate with industries in areas of mutual benefits and for placement and training		
	Any other?		
C6.	**Communication Competencies**		
67.	Develop effective communication channels with internal members and stakeholders for effective performance		
68.	Develop effective feedback mechanisms		
69.	Prepare proposals and reports for various purposes		
70.	Give talks at academic and social functions		
71.	Manage quality electronic and print publications		
	Any other ?		
C7.	**Problem solving Competencies**		
72.	Solve problems for smooth functioning of the institution		

Format 3.2 : (Contd.)

Sl. No.	Competency Profile of Technical Education Manager	Extent of competency	
		Possessed by you	Required by you
73.	Promote participatory and team approaches in the functioning of the institution		
	Any other?		
C8.	**Evaluation Competencies**		
74.	Evaluate the performance of the institution, departments, teams and individuals		
75.	Evaluate the performance of academic programmes and projects		
76.	Use evaluation reports for future academic planning		
77.	Assess impact of various academic programmes on industry and society		
	Any other?		
D.	**FINANCIAL**		
78.	Prepare budgets for supporting institutional plans		
79.	Generate revenue through legal and ethical modes		
80.	Use funds for academic growth and development of the institute		
81.	Use zero based budgeting		
82.	Institute scholarships like freeship, prizes, fellowships, etc.		
83.	Audit and evaluate finances		
	Any other?		
E.	**ADMINISTRATIVE**		
84.	Follow impartial and transparent administration		
85.	Maintain documents		
86.	Scan environment for information generation		
87.	Develop management information system		
88.	Prepare reports of various kinds		
89.	Settle complaints, grievances of staff, students and stakeholders		
90.	Manage time effectively		
91.	Any other?		

1. Did you develop the competencies that you possess now through :

   (a) training, (b) experience, (c) self-learning, and (d) mentoring ? (tick the relevant).

2. Do you think that there is a need to professionally develop above competencies? Yes/No. If yes, list the first 5 competencies that need to be developed.
3. Does the management have training policies for developing requisite competencies through NITTTRs and other training organizations? Yes/No

Format 3.3: *Training Needs of Jail Department*

Sl. No.	*Competencies*	*Functionaries*							
		1	*2*	*3*	*4*	*5*	*6*	*7*	*8*
A.	**Stakeholders**								
1.	Identify significant stakeholders and their stake								
2.	Design strategies to manage stakeholders for the benefit of the department								
3.	Manage stakeholders for the benefit of the department								
B.	**Role Derivation**								
4.	Derive roles of different functionaries in changing context								
5.	Identify role related conflict and stress								
6.	Design strategies to manage role related stress								
7.	Enrich role of different functionaries in changing context								
C.	**Managerial**								
8.	Depict appropriate leadership behaviour in different situations								
9.	Prepare plans for introducing reforms in the jail								
10.	Take effective decisions								
11.	Solve problems								
12.	Manage conflicts								
13.	Manage crisis								
14.	Foster effective communication								
15.	Guide and counsel staff								
16.	Introduce various government schemes in the jail								
17.	Foster healthy interpersonal relationship among employees								
18.	Foster healthy interpersonal relationship among prisoners								
19.	Project good image of the jail in public using various modes								

***Format 3.3* : (*Contd.*)**

Sl. No.	*Competencies*	*Functionaries*							
		1	*2*	*3*	*4*	*5*	*6*	*7*	*8*
20.	Monitor the activities of the jail and take remedial actions on day-to-day basis								
21.	Work in teams								
22.	Ensure hygienic conditions in the Jail								
23.	Plead the case in various organizations such as Court, Human Rights Commission, Women Commission, SC and ST Commission etc.								
24.	Evaluate the performance of various activities and schemes and take corrective actions								
25.	Manage inventory of items for running day-to-day activities								
26.	Build trust in the Jail								
D.	**Information Technology**								
27.	Develop plans to introduce IT in functioning of the jail								
28.	Use management information system (MIS) for various purposes								
29.	Develop e-copy of all documents								
30.	Use IT for various purposes in the Jail								
E.	**Research**								
31.	Conduct surveys on various issues related to prisoners and functioning of the jail								
32.	Support research studies conducted by other organization and research scholars								
33.	Conduct Jail audit								
F.	**Training and Development**								
34.	Identify training needs of the employees to meet the requirements of changing needs of the Jail								
35.	Develop training materials on live situations to make the training programmes purposeful								
36.	Design training programmes for prisoners for various purposes								
37.	Organize training programmers for prisoners in collaboration with different stakeholders								
38.	Use modern arms and ammunition								

A Case Study

Developing a Competency Framework for Government Department

One of the State governments wanted to systematize the training and development interventions for employees of all the departments. So it requested the State training academy to evolve a model of identifying the training needs that can be used by rest of the departments. It requested the academy to evolve model which is participative and can be used by training managers of respective departments. The objective of the study was to develop the competency profile at cutting age level, identify the training and non-training interventions and later on design and implement competency based training programmes using various modes.

The State academy invited the experts working in resource institutions who have experience of conducting such studies. It organized a two days duration workshop of experts and representatives of selected participating departments to prepare a road map for conducting the study. The highlights of road map are stated below :

- The academy and experts will facilitate the design and conduction of study. A team of resource persons from the respective departments will take lead to conduct the study under the guidance of the expert team and resource persons.
- The academy will facilitate the team using various approaches such as orientation and development of the team to design and conduct the study, guide and support as and when needed, monitoring and problem solving, conducting training programmes and workshop with different purposes, supporting data collection, analysis and drawing conclusions and report writing.
- Providing secretarial support such as recording the minutes, documenting the outcomes of the workshop, maintain record of correspondence and mobilizing resources at different locations at all phases of the study.

The road map was prepared for capacity and capability building of government department with following objectives :

- Professionally design HR interventions.
- Identify behavioural, motivational and environmental areas for performance improvement.
- Design need based training interventions.

- Create awareness of designing and conducting systematic training and development programmes.
- Develop competency based flexible and independent training modules.
- Derive roles considering present and future requirements of the department.
- List and analyze jobs and tasks.
- Derive competency profile for different position holders.
- Conduct competency survey and identify the gaps.

The academy used following implementation strategy to achieve the objectives of developing the model.

Initial Workshop

A workshop of experts and resource persons was organized to develop the model which can be followed by all the departments of the State. The significant outcomes of the workshop were as follows :

Meeting with Department

The head of department, training manager, and resource persons from department were invited to brief them about the project, its dimensions, purposes, efforts and time required from the department etc. The department constituted a team for the purpose with a designated team leader.

Workshop on deciding Methodology of the Study

The academy conducted a workshop of the departmental team to decide the methodology to conduct the research study. The duration of workshop was kept three days. The output of the workshop is stated below :

- The team members were educated on organizational visioning, diagnosis, training needs analysis, tools and techniques of training needs analysis, instrument design, observation, conducting interview and other related topics to complete the study.

- The team conducted brainstorming session before deciding the methodology of the study. The team members generated ideas such as training need analysis is not one time activity, it should be done at department level in decentralized manner, the aim should be capacity and capability building. It should be helpful to develop the healthy culture and improve performance of the department as a whole, should be supported by training needs analysis guide and manual. The manual should be prepared on points such as introduction to training needs analysis, its purpose, models of training needs analysis, methodology, population, sample size, method of selecting the sample, design of instruments and guidelines to use them, mode of data collection, data analysis, interpretations and recommendation, training needs and non-training needs.
- *TNA Models :* The team decided to use organizational diagnosis and role derivation model, Boydell model of implementing, improving and innovating model, visioning model, key performance area, performance appraisal and development model, and strengths, weaknesses, opportunities and threats analysis model. The trainers introduced all these models to the team which was followed by discussion on method of using these models in designing the study. The team used these models and came out with vision, missions and goals of the department, strengths, weaknesses, opportunities and threats, improvement and innovative initiatives to be immediately designed and implemented, significant problems related to performance of the department and broad strategies at department level.
- *Tools and Techniques:* The team decided to use role derivation, job analysis, task analysis tools for significant functionaries. The team designed a comprehensive instrument to study the department and its functionaries. The instruments were designed on the basis of output of various models in the context of department and tools and techniques. The instruments were tried out on selected sample and refined based on the comments of the respondents and experts. The details of instruments are stated in the following Table:

Tools	*Parameter*	*Respondent*	*Technique*
Information sheet for department	• Objectives of department, • Number of different functionaries, • Five significant performance problems, • Five priority areas of functioning and training implication, • Availability of training policy, programme of action, departmental manual and training material, • Main focus of the department, • Existing training infrastructure, training programmes conducted, training material developed and support received from different resource organizations.	Department head and training manager	Format filling
Structured interview schedule	• Actual job description of the subordinate, • Significant problems faced by subordinate, • Job related training imparted to subordinate, • Work norms, • Interest in imparting training, • Training needs in basic areas such as office procedure, record management, project management, use of computer, guidance, counseling, mentoring, problem solving and decision making, time management, working in a team, • Work related complaints about subordinate, • Suggestions to remove complaints, • Attention paid by subordinate on parameters such as time dead line, safety, involvement, quality of service, speed of work, accountability, • Mode of training to be used formal, on the job, distance learning,	Immediate superior	Interview of the functionary

Tools	*Parameter*	*Respondent*	*Technique*
	• Work related expectations from subordinates.		
Structured interview schedule	• Problems faced working with colleague, • Challenges in work, • Training needs of colleagues, • Improvement of performance after receiving training, • Work related expectations.	Colleagues	Interview
Structured interview schedule	• Problems faced working with superior, • Training imparted by superior and areas of training, • Training needs of superior, • Work related expectations from superior.	Subordinate	Interview
Structured interview schedule	• Services received from department, • Problems faced in receiving the services, • Satisfaction level, • Reasons of dissatisfaction, • Improvements in services desired, • Training needs of officials, • Significant expectations from department.	Customers and stakeholders	Interview
Structured interview schedule	• Work experience, • Significant jobs, responsibilities, and duties performed, • Significant work related Training needs to solve problems or improve performance, • Use of technology and techniques to improve the perfomance, • Self initiatives to enhance the effectiveness and efficiency in performance, • Progress assessment and feedback received, • Existence of performance standards • Need of significant and immediate steps to improve the performance of the department,	Job holder	Interview Format filling

Tools	*Parameter*	*Respondent*	*Technique*
	• Challenges foreseen in providing services, • Details of recent training received, • Work related complaints received, • Ways to improve personal effectiveness and efficiency, • Need of job redesign to save time, cost and efforts, • Role dependency on other functionaries, • Reasons of satisfaction or dissatisfaction, • Training needs of superior, • Competency survey of job-holder using competency statements, their level of involvement, difficulty in performance and level of avoidance.		
Observation sheet	The trained team observed the behaviour of different functionaries in their natural work setting without informing them on criteria such as time management, work planning, work method, problems solving, use of resources, communication, leadership and followership, team work, accomplishment of objectives, work quality and beneficiary satisfaction.	Job holder	Observation

The team developed the competency profile at functionary level based on the outputs of models and use of tools and techniques. These competencies were further validated by representatives of functionaries, superiors, subordinates and experts.

Training : The team members were trained to collect the information using the tools and techniques. The team members visited selected four districts of the State and collected information using instruments.

Workshop : The information was compiled, classified, and interpreted by the team under the guidance of resource persons. The complete process of the study was recorded in a written report. The report was presented to the Head of department and other significant persons to use it for designing and implementing training programmes and taking decisions on non-training interventions.

The competency profile developed for project officer integrated child and development scheme (ICDS) is given below :

Legend: I – Involvement, D – Difficulty and A – Avoidance

Sl. No.	*Competency statements*	I	D	A
1.	Plan project services according to local situation.			
2.	Communicate project services to various stakeholders like beneficiaries, social groups, non-government organization, health department, etc.			
3.	Solve project related problems.			
4.	Establish linkages with stakeholders.			
5.	Observe rules and regulations related to ICDS.			
6.	Assess the progress of ICDS.			
7.	Verify records maintained by supervisors, assistant statistical officer and Anganwadi workers.			
8.	Maintain records and reports related to ICDS.			
9.	Ensure effective functioning of supervisors, assistant statistical officer and Anganwadi workers.			
10.	Prepare various types of reports to be submitted to various agencies.			
11.	Involve various social groups in the project.			
12.	Mobilize community support to sustain the benefits of the project.			
13.	Impart need based training to various ICDS functionaries.			
14.	Lead various publicity and aware campaign for different government schemes.			
15.	Accomplish project objectives such as reducing pregnant women death rate, child death rate, malnutrition rate, etc.			
16.	Contribute in other government schemes such as Pulse polio, eradication of measles, family planning, *Padna Badna*, etc.			
17.	Use computer for data management and other project related activities.			

10. Review Questions

1. Explain Iceberg model of competency.
2. Describe the process of developing a competency framework for an organization which is not having it.

3. Define competency cluster and state its significance in developing competency profile.
4. List the use of competency profile in managing HR processes.
5. State the difference between competency framework, competency profile and competency map.
6. State the use of competency profile.

11. Activities for HR Managers

Activity 3.1: Audit the competency framework of your organization using Format 1.1 and suggest suitable strategies to make it more relevant and purposeful.

Activity 3.2: Suggest an approach for developing competency framework for an organization which is working traditionally and shown interest to implement the competency framework for managing HR processes.

Activity 3.3: Consider the profile of position holders who have largest population and are working at cutting edge level in your organization. Classify their competencies on various parameters such as essential, desirable, optional, routine, non-routine, critical, innovative, etc.

Activity 3.4: Conduct a training needs analysis survey using competency profile for different position holders. You can use the format as stated in Format 1.2. Analyze the results of competency survey and identify the training needs, prioritize them and communicate to training department.

Activity 3.5: Design a competency based training programme based on the training needs analysis report for particular position holders.

Activity 3.6: Assess the potential of individuals for acquiring various competencies related to their role.

Activity 3.7: Collect the following information for developing competency framework:

- Vision, missions, goals and objectives of organization.
- Customers for different products and services.
- Products and services and market share of each.
- Stakeholders and their stake.
- Major core strengths.
- Significant challenges.

- Major weaknesses.
- Significant threats.
- Major opportunities.
- Main competitors.
- Organizational structure.
- Core functions and roles.
- Main policies and their effectiveness.
- Significant complaints of customers.
- Main grievances of employees.
- Effectiveness of communication channels.
- Role description of key functionaries.
- Significant achievements of previous three years.
- Major changes introduced in last three years.

4

Tools and Techniques for Competency Framework Development

LEARNING OBJECTIVES

After reading this chapter the readers will be able to :

- State the need and importance of using tools and techniques for developing the competency framework.
- List various types of tools and techniques used for competency framework development.
- Describe tools and techniques used in developing competency framework.
- List various sources of secondary information.

1. Introduction

The competency framework development is a research approach. The research is completed using scientifically designed tools and techniques. As mentioned earlier the competency framework is used for designing all types of HR interventions so that all the tools, techniques, approaches and strategies used for managing the human resources are directly or indirectly contribute for competency development. In this chapter a basket of tools and techniques is briefly described. These tools and techniques can be appropriately selected for developing the competency framework for a particular organization. The data, facts and information gathered and generated will be useful for not only developing the competency framework but it will also be useful for designing, implementing and evaluating various types of HR interventions.

2. Tools and Techniques for Developing and Using Competency Framework

There are numbers of tools and techniques used for developing competency framework. These are used for reducing the time and efforts required in developing and producing perfect competency framework. The use of tools and techniques depends on the purpose of developing the competency framework. If it is developed with an objective of institution building, implementing innovation at organization level, and reengineering HR processes then a basket of variety of tools and techniques are used to arrive at competency framework. Some of the significant tools and techniques are briefly described in subsequent paragraphs.

3. Organization Diagnosis Tools and Techniques

Organization Deficiency and Role Derivation

This approach is used to identify the gaps in performance of the organization on critical success factors. The gaps are analyzed to design the strategies and identify the competencies to be developed in different functionaries. The role of significant functionaries is derived using theory of expectancy analysis and derived role is compared with current job of the functionaries. The gap between role and job is also used for developing competency framework and competency profile. The gap is fulfilled designing HR interventions.

Visioning Approach

The organization wide creativity sessions are conducted to craft the vision of the organization. The focus of visioning is to understand future business, thrust, and prepare the employees to accept the challenges. The output of visioning exercises becomes the base for developing vision reach strategies. The vision, missions, values, vision reach strategies, strengths, weaknesses, opportunities and threats, current HR policies and practices, project plans, expectations of customers and stakeholders etc. provide significant information for writing competencies required in employees to achieve the vision. The visioning exercises are powerful tools and techniques to develop creativity of employees, make them aware about future expectations, design collective and individual goals and develop them to perform changing role.

SWOT Analysis

Strengths, weaknesses, opportunities and threats analysis is used to identify the strengths and weaknesses of the organization on various parameters such as human resources profile, HR processes, core processes, assets of organization, quality of products and services and so on. The output of strengths and weaknesses analysis is useful in identifying competencies required to fill up the current gaps. Similarly, the analysis of opportunities and threats on various dimensions such as social, technological, economical and political is carried out. The output of opportunity and threats analysis is useful for designing strategies to grab the opportunities, and minimize and prevent the threats. The vision reach stratcgies are the source of competencies required in near future.

Adopt

There are many organizations in similar business that are performing well. They may be competitors as well as sister organizations. Study the competency framework developed by them to find its purposes, benefits, problems of implementation and impact on the business. This framework can be modified, refined and adopted for various purposes. It is implemented and results are assessed for its effectiveness. If it produces expected results it is continued otherwise further fine tuned.

4. Reviewing Techniques

These techniques are used to review the various processes and products of the organization for holistic understanding of the business of the organization and its future intents. The following process and documents are reviewed to record the strengths and weaknesses. The processes and products are improved on the basis of analysis of information and conclusions.

Plans of the Organization

The HR team reviews all the plans such as strategic plan, perspective plan, operational plan and project plans of the organization to understand its vision, missions, goals, strategies, shift in business, desired values and culture, major expansions and changes in business, product and the like. The information gathered through review of plans is used for crafting the competencies required in near future to implement change and innovations. It is used for updating the competency framework and competency profile at organizational level. It is also used for designing and implementing HR interventions related to training and development, deployment and redeployment, succession planning and so on.

Roles and Responsibilities

There are numbers of organizations who have not crafted roles and responsibilities for different positions. Employees are performing based on the old practices and traditions. In such situations the development of competency framework is difficult and will not bring much of impact for improving the performance. In such situations the team uses role derivation exercise and then work on role analysis for developing competency framework.

If the role of the employees is well designed then role survey should be conducted to assess the effectiveness of their role and its impact on the performance of the organization. A sample list of criteria and format for role satisfaction survey of teachers is suggested in Format 4.1. The role is the base for developing competency profile for different positions so roles are classified under various role dimensions and clusters in each dimension. The priority of role dimension on a particular role is also fixed considering the role requirement. For example the major role dimension of lecturers is teaching-learning on which all the lecturers perform and devote major efforts and time. In developing competency profile for lecturers more emphasis is given on the competencies related to teaching learning process.

Documents

All types of documents such as plans, reports, news letters, logbook, correspondence, annual report etc. are produced at different points of time. They are the secondary source of information. Information collected through review of these documents helps in identifying the trends, problems, issues, experiences, achievements, core competence etc. The information gathered through these documents is useful to derive the competencies and design HR interventions.

Study Critical Incidences

The HR team studies the critical incidences of the organization, teams, and individuals on various aspects of the business. It records the competency requirements to deal with adverse situations or induct the extraordinary talent in main stream. This study helps in making the competency framework holistic and gap free.

5. Information Gathering Tools

The information related to many aspects of performance is need to be collected and analyzed for developing the competency framework. The tools and techniques used for information gathering are briefly described below.

Interview Schedule

The interview schedules are designed and used to gather the views of governing body, stakeholders and significant functionaries on various current and future aspects of the business, future plans, HR challenges, type and level of competition, strengths and weaknesses, policies and functioning of the organization. The structured interview schedules are designed by team and interviews are conducted by trained team members. The data and information are classified, analyzed and used for developing the competency framework, competency profiles and designing HR interventions.

Rating Scales

These are designed for various purposes such as gathering the views of employees on certain issues, functioning of the organization, norms of functioning, problems in performance, role and job allocation, training, guidance and mentoring facility, incentives and grievances. The views, data and information are classified, analyzed, and used for developing the competency framework, competency profiles and designing HR interventions. Rating scales are used for bringing objectivity in subjectivity and quantity in quality.

Observation Schedule

These are designed to study and assess the current practices, technology, competencies, norms, behaviour, culture etc. for framing the competencies and deciding proficiency level. The information gathered through observation is primary, authentic, and relevant. So it is used for setting the benchmarks and designing and implementing HR interventions.

Focused Group Discussion

The team invites the experts of various disciplines of the business of the organization and organizes focus group discussion on significant issues, HR trends, future expectations of customers and stakeholders and so on. The outcomes of discussions are recorded for referring and developing competency framework. Similar focused group discussions are organized drawing significant position holders working in the organization that influences the business of the organization. Their views are important for developing the competency framework.

Creativity Techniques

These are frequently used at every stage for developing competency framework. The team should be trained to conduct creativity sessions with a purpose to generate enough ideas to take effective decisions. Some creativity techniques such as brain storming, nominal group technique and concept mapping are predominantly and frequently used by the team. These techniques are used where the issue is known to team but enough information and solution is not available.

Search Conference

These are becoming popular because of their inherent strengths of seeking the benefit of experiences, creativity and expectations of all those who are concerned for the betterment of the business, quality of products and services, efficiency of production and satisfaction of internal and external stakeholders. The representative sample from all the cadres is drawn and they are taken away from the work situation. They generate ideas on all the issues flagged to them related to business of the organization. If the scope of competency framework is wide in such situations representatives from sister organizations also participate. The professional body or the association of similar industries uses search conference approach for developing generic and common competency framework which can further be elaborated by individual organization.

Secondary Information

The organizations produce number of documents for various purposes. These documents provide information for framing the competency framework at organizational level and competency profile at role level. These documents are as follows :

- All types of plans prepared at organizational, departmental, section, team and individual level.
- All types of reports generated for various purposes such as periodic report, progress report, annual report, failure report, audit report, performance appraisal report, training report, research report etc.
- All types of feedback generated by internal as well as external customers.
- All types of extraordinary records such as change management documents, certification documents, work manuals, policy manual, quality guidelines, training material etc.
- Problem analysis records maintained at different levels.
- Analysis of customer complaints and suggestions.
- Critical incidences recorded by superiors.

6. Summary

- The competency framework development is a research approach. It is completed using scientifically designed tools and techniques.
- The data, facts and information generated using tools and techniques are useful for developing the competency

framework and designing, implementing and evaluating various types of HR interventions.

- There are numerous tools and techniques such as organization deficiency and role derivation model, visioning approach, SWOT analysis, adopting the competency framework of similar organization, etc. The reviewing techniques are used to take out data from plans, roles, responsibilities, documents, critical incidences, etc.
- Techniques used for developing competency framework are interview, rating, observation, focus group discussion, creativity, search conferences, analysis of information etc.
- Tools and techniques are used for reducing the time and efforts required in developing competency framework and producing perfect competency framework.
- The use of tools and techniques depends on purpose of developing competency framework.

7. Formats

Format 4.1: *Role Satisfaction Survey for Teachers*

The role satisfaction inventory is designed to measure the role satisfaction level of principals of schools. This inventory can be used for teachers and other significant employees. Please indicate your response on various dimensions of role satisfaction. You can indicate +3 for very high satisfaction, +2 for high satisfaction and +1 for satisfaction, 0 for not sure, –1 for low dissatisfaction, –2 for high dissatisfaction, and –3 for very high dissatisfaction in column 3 (level of satisfaction/dissatisfaction). Please write brief description of the causes/reasons of dissatisfaction in column 4. Then identify and write strategies to remove dissatisfaction in column number 5. If the role satisfaction level is very high or high in such case the competencies are identified and competency profile is drawn. The training and development needs are identified to further enrich the role. If the role satisfaction level is low first the management strategy such as role enrichment, role rotation, identification of potential and training to harness the potential are used. Then competency profile is drawn for designing further HR strategies.

Role Satisfaction Survey for Teachers

Sl. No.	*Role dimensions*	*Level of satisfaction/ dissatisfaction*	*Description and causes of dissatisfaction*	*Strategies to remove dissatisfaction*
1	*2*	*3*	*4*	*5*
1.	My role matches with my competence			
2.	My role matches with my interest			
3.	My role is challenging			
4.	My role provides me time to regain energy			
5.	My role provides me opportunity to select higher order goals after a period of time			
6.	My school provides me an opportunity for training as and when required			
7.	My school solves role related problems			
8.	My role demands for creativity			
9.	My school provides me an opportunity to plan the role			
10.	My role provides me an opportunity to perform variety of tasks			
11.	My school provides necessary resources on time to perform the role			
12.	My school assesses the competence and potential using variety of methods			
13.	My school assigns me new assignments/ projects			
14.	My school rewards excellent performance			
15.	My school has healthy culture to facilitate role performance			
16.	My school provides an opportunity for self-development			

Format 4.1: (Contd.)

Sl. No.	Role dimensions	Level of satisfaction/ dissatisfaction	Description and causes of dissatisfaction	Strategies to remove dissatisfaction
1	2	3	4	5
17.	My school has empowered me to perform the role taking appropriate decisions at right time			
18.	My role is designed in tune with the other roles in the school and there is no role conflict, role overlap, role encroachment, role gap etc.			
19.	My role provides me an opportunity to work in a team			
20.	My role is core role in the school			
21.	There is enough scope for delegation of routine role dimensions in my school			
22.	There is a provision of providing informal and formal feedback for improving the performance on role			
23.	People hold accountable for non-performance			
24.	There is equal distribution of role in the school			
25.	People get an opportunity to generate ideas to improve the performance			

8. Review Questions

1. State three importance of using tools and techniques in developing competency framework.
2. List two indirect benefits of using tools and techniques for developing competency framework.
3. Describe the process of developing competency framework using organization deficiency and role derivation model.

4. Describe the process of visioning for developing competency framework. Which competencies are identified using this model?
5. State the purpose of SWOT analysis for developing competency framework.
6. State five limitations of adopting a competency framework for similar organization.
7. Explain the process of analyzing organizational plans for developing competency framework.
8. Explain the process of identifying competencies from role and responsibility analysis.
9. State three purposes of document analysis for developing competency framework.
10. State three strengths and two limitations of interview technique for developing competency framework.
11. List the types of competencies that are identified using rating scale.
12. List five competencies that are identified using observation in your organization context.
13. Describe the process of conducting focus group discussion for developing competency framework.
14. State the conditions in which creativity techniques are used for developing competency framework.
15. Describe the conditions in which search conferences are recommended for developing the competency framework.
16. State three uses of secondary information for developing the competency framework.

9. Activities for HR Managers

Activity 4.1: Design a process and instruments for conducting organization deficiency and role derivation exercise for developing competency framework.

Activity *4.2*: Use vision document of your organization and develop competency framework.

Activity 4.3: Design instruments for conducting SWOT analysis for developing competency framework.

Activity 4.4: Gather competency framework of similar organization and modify it to suit to your organization.

Activity 4.5: Use various documents and identify competencies at organization level for developing competency framework.

Activity 4.6: Conduct interview to identify the competencies for performing a particular role.

Activity 4.7: Observe functioning of various processes and identify competencies.

Activity 4.8: Conduct a focused group discussion for developing competency framework.

Activity 4.9: Use Delphi technique for developing competency framework.

Activity 4.10: Conduct a search conference for developing competency framework.

5

Assessment of Competency

LEARNING OBJECTIVES

After reading this chapter the readers will be able to :

- State the need and importance of assessment of competency.
- State the concept of competency assessment.
- Explain the characteristics of assessment.
- Describe the types of assessment.
- List the factors affecting assessment.
- State the importance of involving stakeholders in assessment.
- State assessment guidelines.
- List competencies of assessors.
- Describe the shift required in assessment.

1. Introduction

The measurement of competency is essential for assessing the competency of individuals for various purposes as stated in Chapter 2. The assessment of competency is carried out with a purpose. If the organization is planning to design a major change in the core business then the purpose of assessment is holistic means the competencies of all the professionals are assessed to achieve the goals of the change. For example, the organization is going for automated production or computerization or on-line marketing or on-line learning or expanding the product features, or diversifying from the current core business or entering into service business etc. In such conditions the competency framework of the organization is evaluated along with competency profile of individuals. If the organization is planning to systematize its training activities the purpose of competency assessment may be identification of training needs. In this situation the purpose is narrow.

2. Concept of Competency Assessment

The competency assessment in organizational context is different than educational context. In educational context the threshold competency is assessed and certified but in organizational context the competency is assessed with a purpose to deploy the employee for productive performance. It is a systematic and scientific process of measuring the role related behaviour of the professional in real life situation against well defined criteria using variety of appropriate methods.

The professionals are given an opportunity to demonstrate the competency and proficiency in real life situation and it is measured using appropriate tools, techniques and criteria. The criteria used for measurement of competency are objective, direct and significant. Generally these criteria are declared before the measurement so only those employees participate who are confident that they can demonstrate the competency up to predefined performance standards. The employees can produce past evidences of demonstrating the competency and proficiency.

3. Characteristics of Assessment

The assessment process should be well designed and fulfil characteristics illustrated in Fig. 5.1. [adopted Gupta, 2007].

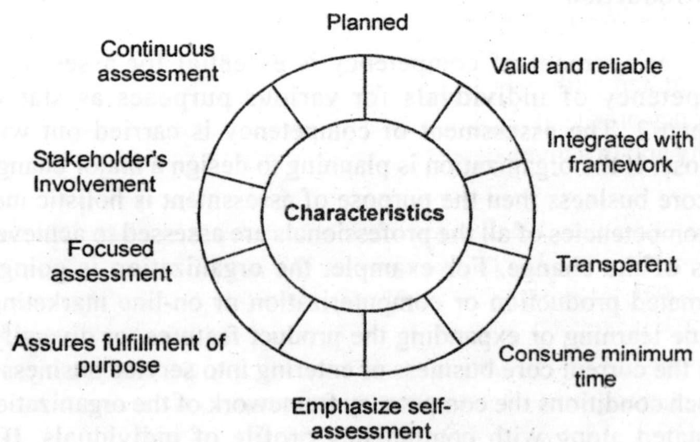

Fig. 5.1 : Characteristics of Assessment

Well Designed

The assessment tools and techniques are designed using scientific approach. The assessors indicate them in the assessment strategy. The criteria for assessment emanates from the essential/core and desirable/peripheral competencies. The assessors derive the parameters from assessment criteria of competency. The integrated assessment reduces the waste of time, money and efforts in assessment process. It reduces the complaints of employees about assessment. The assessment is a planned and continuous activity in competency based human resources interventions.

Valid and Reliable

The assessment tools, methods and procedures are used in a valid and reliable way. They are objectively designed and free from biases and errors. They are designed to assess the significant and important parameters of performance of the competency and not the trivial and irrelevant. The employee collects sufficient evidences of performing the competency during the process of performance in order to self assess the competency and confidently demonstrate the competency before the assessors.

Integrated with Competency Framework

It is integrated with competency framework of the organization and competency profile of the individuals in order to assess the competency in totality and in a given context. Instead of putting more emphasis on assessment alone, assessment is made an integral part of the planning, designing and implementing the process. Inbuilt assessment activity will automatically avoid, prevent, and minimize the limitations of conventional methods of assessment. The assessment is a natural process and is blended naturally with the performance. The assessment tools and techniques are designed and used during performance. The superiors or other stakeholders may use them to assess the competency in natural setting. The assessment tools are designed on the basis of competency to be assessed. The assessment plan is understood and interpreted in the same way by the organization, assessors, assessees and decision makers.

Transparent

The assessment scheme, tools, and techniques are designed and declared at the time of registering for the assessment. The employees know the criteria and method of assessment. It provides them an opportunity to prepare according to the expectations of the assessors. The transparency in assessment helps the employees to elevate their self-expectations and effectively learn to achieve competency.

Consume Minimum Time

The assessment is an integral part of the performance so it consumes considerably less time of employee and assessors. It is not merely assessment but it helps to improve the performance as a whole. It also helps to solve the individual performance problems of the employees. In other words, this type of assessment is more productive.

Emphasis on Self-Assessment

The self-assessment and peer assessment is encouraged in the assessment process. It helps in competency measurement and development because the employees realize that assessment is purposeful and meaningful. Self and peer assessment of competency make them more responsible for performance. They feel accountable for performance. Often they will correct themselves without superiors' interventions. The assessment of competency is one of the significant competencies of professionals. This competency is developed in them through self-assessment and mutual assessment.

Assures Purpose

The ultimate purpose of competency assessment is to assure the purpose. The organization can take appropriate decisions at right time for developing the competencies or hiring the person for a specific job with particular competencies. The organization can know the gaps in competency framework or competency profile and design strategies to fulfil the gaps designing various interventions.

Focused Core Competency Assessment

The assessment focuses on core and higher order competencies in different dimensions of role performance. It focuses more on performance aspects. The assessors identify strong and direct indicators of demonstration of competency and prepare assessment tools. The assessment process results in competency profile of employees against the required competency standards that establishes the overall ability of the employee.

Stakeholders Involvement

The stakeholders are involved in the assessment process. The involvement of stakeholders in assessment increases their common understanding about the assessment that leads to commitment for assessment. The involvement of more number of persons helps in ensuring unbiased assessment. Involvement of more number of persons in the assessment process prevents unnecessary litigation. The assessment related problems are solved amicably leading to healthy assessment of competency.

Continuous Assessment

The continuous or formative assessment continues with the progress in work performance. The cumulative result of assessment is sufficient evidence for certifying the competency. The cumulative results of assessment are compiled and conclusions are drawn at the end of the project or process. There could be many aspects of competency that cannot be assessed at the end of the performance so formative assessment is not to be missed. The records of formative performance appraisal provide evidences for formative assessment. Even it can be clubbed with formative appraisal. The employee maintains the record of progress of work.

4. Types of Assessment

The assessment is carried out with a specific purpose in a given context. The assessment can be classified on various criteria stated in Fig. 5.2.

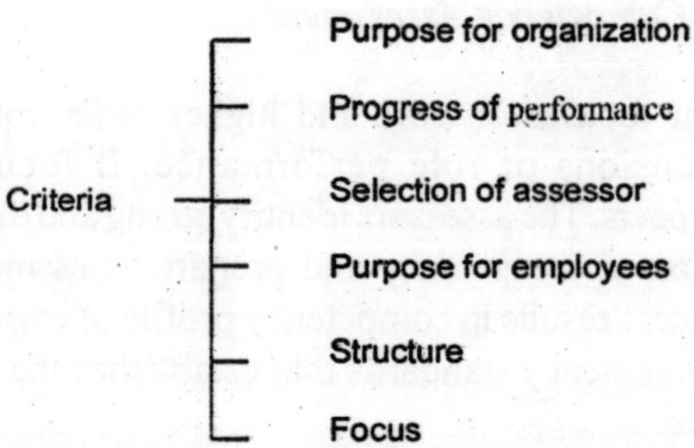

Fig. 5.2 : Criteria of Classifying Assessment

According to Purpose for Organization

According to purpose for organization the assessment of competency is carried out for recruitment, redeployment, promotion, training, giving rewards, role enrichment, etc.

According to Progress of Performance

According to progress of performance the assessment is classified as formative and summative as stated in Fig 5.3 and described in subsequent paragraphs.

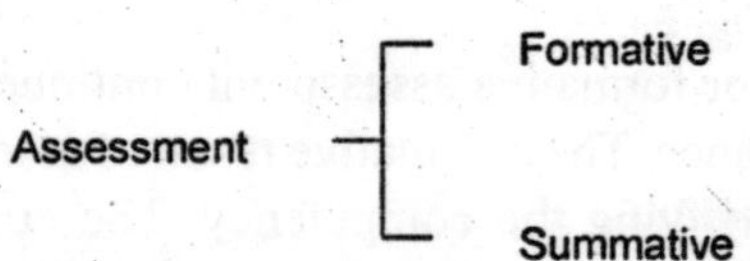

Fig. 5.3 : According to Progress of Performance

Formative Assessment

It is an integral process of assessment in the performance. Superiors as well as new employees carry out the assessment in natural performance setting. The assessment is a part and partial of performance so no extra efforts are required on the part of the superiors as well as employees. The formative assessment is used by superiors to provide positive and constructive feedback to new employees for refining the competency with reference to assigned role. It is used to refine on the job training, guidance, counseling and coaching in order to refine competency and proficiency of employees.

Summative Assessment

It is carried out after the completion of project or achievement of goals. It is used to assess the level of achievement of individuals on particular assignment. It is also carried out to identify the potential of employee for performing a new role. It is carried out against predefined criteria of assessment of competency that is required to perform new role. Independent assessors who are not associated with supervision of individual performance carry out the summative assessment of core competencies. This approach increases objectiveness and fairness in assessment of the competencies.

According to Selection of Assessors

According to selection of assessors the assessment is classified as internal and external as stated in Fig 5.4 and described in subsequent paragraphs.

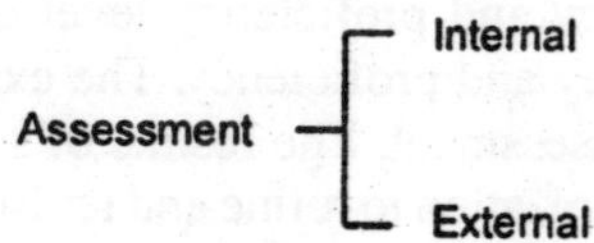

Fig. 5.4 : According to Selection of Assessor

Internal Assessment

It is carried out by the superiors to keep track on the progress of performance according to roles, responsibilities and duties. It is used to diagnose the performance problems and solve them effectively at right time. It is used for providing peer feedback for improving the performance and empowering the employees for self-monitoring the progress and realizing the responsibility for performance. It is also carried out to facilitate the competency refinement process of employees. Generally, supervisors carry out formative assessment. The internal assessment is influenced by halo effect, biases, recent incidences, oversights, leniency, strictness, emotions, and like errors.

Self-assessment is a process of empowering the employees to develop competencies and proficiency on their own. The concept of self-development is predominantly used in learning organizations. The employees are trained to be conscious about self-assessment. Whatever they do, they should reflect on their experiences, and learn out of it. The habit of self-assessment can be increased using variety of assignments such as report writing, making presentation, participating in a game, attempting case study, working on project, and the like.

Peer assessment is equally important in internal assessment. Employees devote maximum time with their colleagues in the organization. The colleagues are the strong and rich sources for providing assessment of almost all the competencies. They naturally observe the life style and offer comment, suggestions, critiques, opinions, feedback, remarks, jokes, etc. in positive and negative manner. It is a kind of assessment that can be used by employees for improvement. Superiors formally offer feedback during meetings, discussions and performance.

External Assessment

Assessors called from outside the organization carry it out. They are generally drawn from education, training, and certifying agency. They assess the competency and proficiency level of the employees and certify the competency and proficiency. The external assessors carry out the summative assessment. The results of summative assessment are useful for the organization to refine and revise the human resources interventions. The organization can also ascertain the level of effectiveness of the training and development activities.

The external assessment is used to maintain minimum level of competency of employees. It is free from emotions, feelings, and biases. The external assessment is costly and time consuming. It should be used for taking significant decisions.

According to Purpose for Employee

According to purpose the assessment is carried out to assess the current competencies and know the potential of developing the new competencies. This is helpful in choosing the right role in the same organization or applying for a new position. The industries and companies are facing competitions and challenges. They want to employ right person for right job. They want to select the professionals who can fulfil the changing requirements of the industry. They want to place the people with right kind of attitudes and willing to excel for the benefit of the company.

The assessment for placement is conducted by analyzing the core competencies required for the job and assessing the potential candidates on the basis of the core competencies. Many companies have benchmarked the core competencies for placement of right candidates on job. They assess the candidates against core competencies on assessment criteria and employ them.

According to Structure

According to structure the assessment is classified as formal and informal as stated in Fig 5.5. Both the types of assessment are commonly used in assessing the competencies.

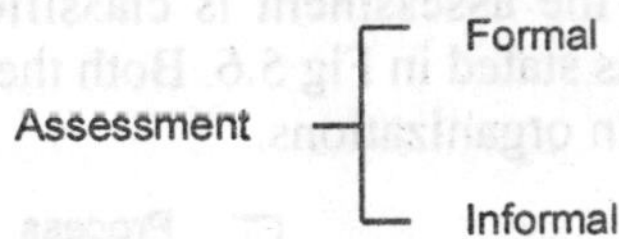

Fig. 5.5 : According to Structure

Formal Assessment

It is a planned, conscious, structured, scheduled, and well-organized activity in which employees consciously respond to the assessment tools. Employees know in advance that they are going to be assessed on competency with a purpose. They know the criteria of assessment and consciously prepare well for the assessment. The formal assessment creates anxiety, tension and even certain level of stress, if it is assessment for placement on higher job, or challenging project, or promotion or significant rewards. The results of formal assessment are reported and recognized. The purpose for which formal assessment is carried out is mentioned in the human resources development policy of the organization.

Informal Assessment

The superiors and colleagues are involved in performance. They often meet and interact at work place. They form an image of a particular employee based on their interaction and observation. This image may be true or biased. Superiors also study the facial expressions and body language of the employees and conclude about the competencies of the employees. They go through the outputs of the tasks and reports to form the opinion about the employees. This is an example of informal assessment. Similarly employees informally interact with each other, observe the activities of each other, analyze the results of interactions and observations to form the image of their colleagues. Similarly employees assess the performance of superiors. The informal assessment is useful in making friendship, forming groups with a purpose, counseling, diagnosing the problem, exploring the potential, and guiding the employees.

According to Focus

According to focus the assessment is classified into process and product assessment as stated in Fig 5.6. Both the types of assessment are commonly used in organizations.

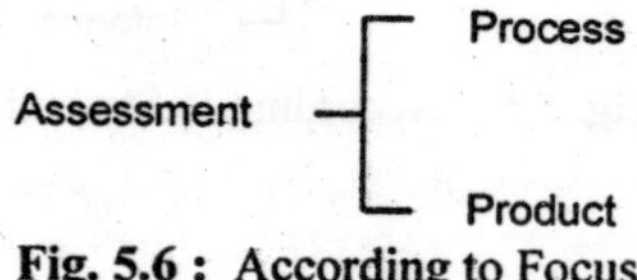

Fig. 5.6 : According to Focus

Process Assessment

In developing and refining competencies in all the three domains of learning the process assessment is very important because the process cannot be replicated time and again. Along with core competency the employees use variety of associative competencies. For example, the employees perform a task on the production line following a set process. Their performance can be assessed on method of completing the task as well as on many other associative competencies, such as reading the drawing, planning the job, selection of tools, observing safety precautions, appropriate use of tools and skills, and the like. Once the process of performing the task is over such competencies cannot be assessed.

Another important point is that inexperienced employees are not professionals, they are learners, so they continuously need feedback on process of performing the task. The process assessment is useful in developing and refining effective domain and psychomotor domain competencies. It is often used in laboratory, workshop, industrial training, project, and role-play. The process assessment is supported by scientifically designed tools and techniques such as check list, observation sheet, rating scale, and the like.

Product Assessment

The employees are expected to demonstrate and use competencies in real life situation. While demonstrating the competencies they produce variety of products such as drawing sheet, report, diary, job, manual, design of product, solution to a problem, strategy to achieve challenging goal, plan to achieve goals, model, case study, and the like. The quality of product is equally important for assessing the level of competency and proficiency. The quality of product speaks a lot about the process of performance. The product assessment is supported by scientifically designed assessment tools such as rating scale, checklist, and observation sheet.

The types of assessment described in preceding paragraphs makes the assessor appreciate the range, depth, breadth, and proficiency required in assessment. The assessment process is designed selecting various types of assessment and packaging them with a purpose.

5. Factors Affecting Assessment

The assessment process is influenced by many and varied factors positively as well as negatively. The indicative factors affecting assessment positively are stated in the following points :

- Scientifically and systematically designed competency framework, profile and competency statement.
- Scientifically designed assessment process for each competency.
- Integrated assessment process with performance.
- Trained superiors and HR persons in assessment.
- Scientifically designed assessment tools and techniques.
- Transparent assessment process.
- Well informed assessment scheme to employees, superior and stakeholders.
- Computerized assessment record management.
- Culture of self-assessment and peer assessment.

Factors affecting assessment negatively are stated in following points:

- Set pattern of assessment.
- Causal approach in assessment.
- No/low use of assessment data for designing HR interventions.
- Purpose of assessment is not clear.
- Completing the formality.
- Biasness in assessment.

6. Involvement of Stakeholders in Assessment Process

The stakeholders play a very important role in the process of assessment. The whole purpose of assessment is to ascertain the level of competency and proficiency for various purposes. The stakeholders are involved in assessment process considering the purposes of the assessment. The stakeholders for assessment are stated in Fig. 5.7 and their role is described in subsequent paragraphs.

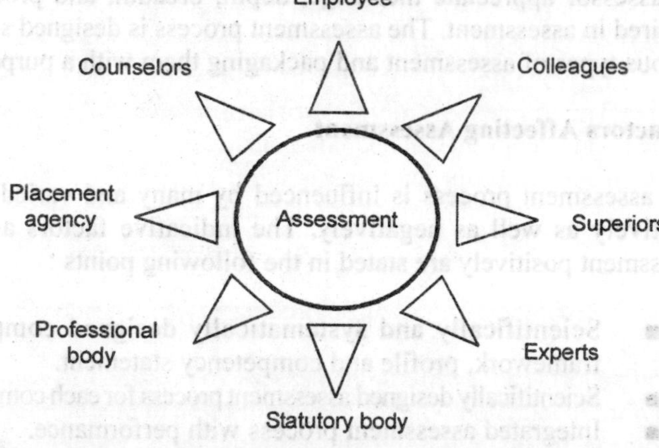

Fig. 5.7 : Stakeholders of Assessment Process

Employees

The scientific approach to assessment will be successful only when the employees and superiors are involved in the assessment process for various purposes such as improving the quality of products and services, effective communication, performance appraisal, redeployment, deciding the incentives, identifying training needs and so on.

Colleagues

Constructive peer feedback plays an important role in improving the performance. It reduces the time of the superiors for assessment at the same time employees are more comfortable in peer assessment. They take the assessment process joyfully because there is no risk in it. The assessor also learns variety of skills during the peer-assessment process. They correct themselves without the intervention of a superior.

Superior

The role of superiors is important in the process of assessment. The assessment rating given by superiors confirms the effectiveness and efficiency in performance. The superiors make unbiased suggestions for improving the performance. The superiors have close association with employees that helps in career advancement, promotion and redeployment.

Experts

The role of the experts is important during the design of the assessment scheme and evaluating the effectiveness of assessment scheme. They communicate the intent and spirit of assessment through training programmes and workshops. The assessment and subject experts may design the assessment scheme for ensuring the development of competency and proficiency, certification of the same, taking decision for training, guiding, counseling and mentoring.

Statutory Body

The involvement of statutory body in assessment process is useful to receive the feedback about the quality of competencies possessed by employees. Their suggestions are also considered to be useful from legal point of view. It becomes the means for collaborating on the activities of mutual benefit. The assessment given by statutory body boosts up the confidence of one and all in the organization for assuring quality of products and services. It helps in enhancing the corporate reputation of the organization.

Professional Body

The involvement of professional body in design of assessment scheme and assessment process helps to update the competency framework and profile to make it appropriate and relevant to the core and changing business of the organization. It helps to assure the quality of manpower for professional performance. There are numerous professional bodies supporting the scientific assessment schemes and extending their cooperation.

Counselors

The counselors play a significant role in the process of assessment. They are the first professionals to take initiatives to explore the potential, preferences, and ambitions of the employees' of the organization. Based on the scientific assessment of potential and preferences of the employees they provide guidance, support and exposure to employees to set and achieve the long term as well as short term career objectives. On one hand, superiors provide the profile of the employee on achievement of the personal objectives or competencies and on other hand the counselors provide the overall profile of the employees. The overall profile of employees is described on parameters such as potential of employee, preferences for life and career, personal vision, talent, personality, unique qualities, hobbies, behavioural problems, and the like. The assessment of employees qualities carried out by counselors is a strong means to develop the employees up to their self-actualization level.

7. Assessment Guidelines

The assessors should observe some important points for planning, implementing, interpreting and using assessment results. The guidelines for assessment are stated in the following points :

- Comprehend the competency framework, competency profile and assessment scheme.
- Plan the assessment of competencies considering the purpose of assessment.
- The criteria for certifying the essential/core competency

should be objective and known to employees in advance when they register for the assessment of competency.

- Translate the assessment criteria in strong and direct parameters/indicators for assessment purpose. These parameters are used to design the assessment instruments.
- Keep in mind the objectives of the assessment for designing the assessment tools and methods. The objectives of assessment are to identify training needs, certify level of competency, identify potential to perform a particular role, etc.
- Design the assessment tools aligned to competency, method and purpose of assessment.
- Do not plan to collect unnecessary and irrelevant information through assessment process. At the same time do not forget to collect essential information that will be considered as main evidence for certifying the competency or ascertaining the level of competency.
- Keep the assessment tools and methods free from personal biases. The assessment should produce necessary and sufficient evidence for certifying the competency, which cannot be measured through product assessment. The evidences include the outcomes of assignment, tasks, exercises, games, projects, problem solving, case study, projects, seminars, etc. The evidences and level of achievement of each employee is recorded. Use full range of assessment tools and techniques.
- Record the performance of employees on formal assessment methods such as test, observation, interview, and *viva voce*.
- Assess the progress on performance during the process of performance and after every significant achievement instead of daily, weekly or monthly bases. Time should be a criterion for assessing the competency when it matters. Use formal and informal assessment process during performance. Use process as well as product assessment.
- The assessment should not create any anxiety, tension, and stress. It should not lead to dispute and litigation. However, it should create challenge and motivation for better performance.
- The nature of assessment method depends on nature of competency. For example, the attitude for safety cannot be

assessed in-group discussion but it can be easily assessed when employees are performing.

- Use results of assessment for guidance, counseling, feedback, training and HR interventions.
- Observe the principles of validity, reliability, fairness, and flexibility.
- The employees must know the assessment context, criteria, purpose of assessment and assessment process.
- The assessment should cover all aspects of performance related to competency in the organization.
- Declare the results of all types and aspects of assessment immediately with a feedback for improvement.
- Provide opportunity for reassessment and appeal for correction, if the employee is dissatisfied with the assessment results.
- Use effective inter-personal and communication skills required in assessment process to avoid stress and anxiety.
- Provide adequate information and support to enable employees to gather reliable evidence to support their claim for accreditation of prior certified competencies.
- Arrange and organize the resources to facilitate the assessment process. The resources may be physical such as discussion room, video camera, or human such as trained assessors to observe the behaviour of employees, or sitting arrangement or work setting. It may be assessment resources such as task, assignment, case study, role description, rules for competition etc.
- Educate the employees that the assessment is a means to refine the competency and it is not an end in itself. If the assessment results are not positive the employees are counseled and remedial opportunities are provided.
- Create opportunities to encourage continuous and informal assessment during performance by peers and self
- Involve other superiors in the department, resource persons, and employees in the design of assessment scheme, its implementation, and certification process.

8. Training of Assessors

Since assessment is a significant activity for designing the HR interventions and taking significant decisions for managing the human resources of the organization assessors need to be trained and certified by competent authority to assess the competencies of employees. They should be trained to acquire following competencies :

- Design assessment scheme for each competency stated in competency framework.
- Design valid and reliable assessment tools and techniques for assessing the competencies.
- State criteria for selecting ready made assessment tools for assessing a particular competency.
- Use variety of tools and techniques for assessing the competency.
- Promote fairness, transparency, and maintain integrity in assessment process.
- Promote self-assessment and peer assessment.
- Use computer software for maintaining records of assessment.
- Interpret the results of assessment to draw conclusions with a purpose.
- Provide positive, constructive and development oriented feedback to employees for improving the performance.
- Guide and counsel employees based on assessment results.
- Conduct/participate in research studies on competency based assessment.

9. Paradigm Shift in Assessment

A paradigm shift is required in assessment process because the traditional assessment processes are having numerous limitations. The assessors and employees devote significant time and efforts for assessment. Therefore, a paradigm shift is required in assessment process as stated in Fig. 5.8.

Fig. 5.8 : Paradigm Shift in Assessment

Parameters	*Current Practices*	*Paradigm Shift Required*
Objective	To assess the performance for training and development, promotion, career advancement and giving incentives	To enrich competency framework and competency profile in order to design HR interventions for bringing change and innovation in the business of the organization

Fig. 5.8 : (*Contd.*)

Parameters	*Current Practices*	*Paradigm Shift Required*
Purpose	Classifying the employees according to achievement problem solving	Development of organization for excellence Ensuring quality of products and services Development of individuals as professional
Approach	Based on traditional approaches of assessment Generic	Assessment integrated with performance, change and development
Focus	Sustaining the performance	Value addition Continuous improvement Benchmarking Self-satisfaction Empowerment of employees
Foundation	Reporting	Developing employees for changing roles Developing advance competencies according to needs
Tools and techniques	Traditional	Integrated to performance Scientifically designed
Resource person	All stakeholders whether trained in assessment or not	Professionals and trained assessors within and outside the organization Trained employees for self and peer assessment
Methods	Rigid Time consuming	Involvement of employees in the assessment methods Empowering
Consequences	Sustenance of performance Performance problems solved	HR interventions designed for change and innovation
After assessment	Management feels tension released	High level of satisfaction Win-win situation

10. Summary

- The measurement of competency is essential for assessing the competency for various purposes.

- The competency assessment in organizational context is different than educational context. In educational context the threshold competency is assessed and certified but in organizational context the competency is assessed with a purpose.
- It is a systematic and scientific process of measuring the role related behaviour of the professional in real life situation against well defined criteria using variety of appropriate methods.
- Professionally managed assessment should be planned. Valid, reliable, integrated with competency framework, transparent, consume minimum time and efforts, emphasize self-assessment, assure fulfilment of purpose, focused assessment, involve stakeholders and continuous assessment.
- The type of assessment is decided according to purpose of assessment.
- The assessment can be formative and summative, internal and external, formal and information, product and process related, etc.
- To make the assessment participative and transparent all relevant stakeholders should be involved in assessment process.
- To make the assessment purposeful well defined process and guidelines should be followed in the organization.
- The assessment should be done by trained assessors only.
- There is a need of total shift in assessment approach in organization.

11. Formats

Format 5.1: *Competency Assessment*

Audit the competency assessment on criteria stated in the table given below. During the process of assessment, if you come across deficiencies/gaps/weaknesses, note down the extent of gap in column 3 and description of the gap in column 4 of the table. After examining the assessment process against each criterion and noting down the deficiencies/gaps/weaknesses think about the strategies to bring improvements in assessment process on various criteria and note down the strategy in column 5. You can think about value additions with respect to the criteria under consideration even if you do not find any weakness and mention it in column 5. Please use following scale for indicating extent of deficiencies/gaps/weaknesses in column 3.

- 5 – indicates very high deficiency/gap/weakness,
- 4 – indicates high deficiency/gap/weakness,
- 3 – indicates medium deficiency/gap/weakness,
- 2 – indicates low deficiency/gap/weakness,
- 1 – indicates very low deficiency/gap/weakness, and
- 0 – indicates no deficiency/gap/weakness.

Competency Assessment

Sl. No.	*Criteria*	*Extent of deficiencies/gaps/ weaknesses/ scope for improvement*	*Description of deficiencies/gaps/ weaknesses/ scope/for improvement*	*Strategies to bring improvement*
1	*2*	*3*	*4*	*5*
1.	Planned assessment			
2.	Valid			
3.	Reliable			
4.	Integrated with competency framework			
5.	Transparent			
6.	Consume minimum time and efforts			
7.	Emphasize self assessment			
8.	Assures fulfilment of purpose			
9.	Focused assessment			
10.	Involvement of stakeholders			
11.	Continuous			
12.	Use of right tools and techniques			
13.	By trained assessors			

12. Review Questions

1. State the concept of assessment of competency.
2. Describe the process of competency assessment.
3. Explain the characteristics of assessment process.
4. State the types of assessment.
5. Distinguish between formative and summative assessment.
6. List the advantages and limitations of external and internal assessors in competency based assessment.
7. State the purposes for which internal assessment is carried out.
8. State the purposes for which external assessment is carried out.
9. State the purposes of self-assessment.
10. Describe the conditions under which self-assessment should be promoted.
11. State the conditions under which assessment by peer is useful.
12. State the conditions under which assessment by experts is beneficial.
13. State the purpose of product assessment.
14. State the purpose of process assessment.
15. State the factors affecting competency assessment.
16. State three purposes of involving various stakeholders in assessment process.

13. Activities for HR Managers

Activity 5.1: Assessment of core competency

Design assessment process and assess a core competency of any role from your organization.

Activity 5.2: *Informal assessment*

Design an assessment tool for informally assessing the performance of a core role in your organization.

Activity 5.3: *Process assessment*

Design an assessment tool for process assessment of performance on competencies of a core role in your organization.

6

Competency Based Recruitment

LEARNING OBJECTIVES

After reading this chapter the readers will be able to :

1. State the need and importance of competency based recruitment.
2. State the need and importance of assessment for recruitment.
3. Describe the use of competencies for selection.
4. Explain the assessment tools and techniques for recruitment and selection.
5. State the factors affecting selection of tools and techniques.

1. Introduction

The recruitment of right persons is very important for any professional organization. The right persons can help the organization to select the right business, set challenging business goals and design right strategy for achieving goals. They can save the money, efforts, and time of the organization in managing the business. They can explore and grab the environmental opportunities for continuous growth and development of the organization. They can build the work culture which is healthy, motivating, and satisfying. They can evolve work methods to assure quality at first time and every time. They can develop the subordinates, team members, and colleagues to excel their best for the professional contribution and at the same time for the satisfaction of the customers, beneficiaries, clients, and stakeholders. They share the responsibility of higher order and readily accept the challenges of the core business.

On the contrary, the incompetent persons create problems for superiors, colleagues, and subordinates. They may commit mistakes that directly affect the quality of the product or services or both. They may negatively influence the behaviour of the fellow members which may result in lower moral. They may spoil the culture of the organization. They may become the liability for the organization and can take the organization to any level of declined performance. The incompetent persons at higher position become the source of stress for everyone. They become the barrier for creative and innovative subordinates.

The over competent persons are also a problem for the organization in many ways. Since there is no challenge for them so their competence is underutilized. Over a period of time they may feel monotony and boredom in the role. They will stop taking interest in the routine work and get dissatisfied in absence of enough challenge. They will think to leave the job as early as possible. It is interesting to note here that an engineering college recruited a retired director of technical education on the post of principal assuming that the retired director's name will attract many aspiring students for taking admission. The college also assumed that the legal matters related to technical education would be smoothly solved. Very soon the management of the college realized that the principal is not taking interest in the functioning of the institution. At the same time the principal has also realized that her competence, expertise, and experiences are not being utilized appropriately. She got frustrated and resigned.

Recruitment is the first process to stop the entry of incompetent or over competent persons in the organization. The recruitment process needs to be designed and carry out professionally. The other processes related to their induction, training, performance appraisal, advancement, and promotion are based on selection process.

The working professionals in the organization are assigned new and different roles. For this purpose their competencies are assessed so that roles can be assigned to right person. Or the competencies can be developed in the person to accept the new role. Over a period of time professionals working in the organization are promoted to take up higher responsibilities. Their screening can be done using scientific assessment methods. If the aspirants are not possessing competencies for the role to be assigned and company has a policy for developing competencies in them through training. The company may assess the potential in aspirants for developing the required competencies.

2. Use of Competencies for Selection

The competencies are used for all types of selections such as recruitment, assigning a project, redeployment, promotion, etc. The selection based on competencies assures that the person has potential, capability and capacity to perform professionally in present and near future. The competencies are derived from the role of the person. The role of the person should be clearly defined in broad terms covering all areas of performance. The effectiveness and efficiency of complete selection process depends on the role description. The poorly defined role leads to inappropriate selection.

For example, if the teachers are to be selected for engineering colleges their role on dimensions such as teaching-learning, curriculum design, assessment of learning, research studies, consultancy, guidance and counseling, development of instructional material, networking with research and resource institutions, extension activities, administrative and managerial activities, project development, entrepreneurship, placement of students and the like is designed. The process of deriving the competencies and criteria for assessment is illustrated in Fig. 6.1.

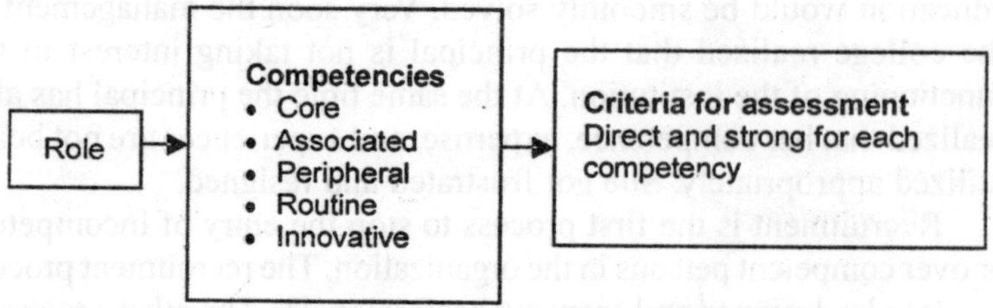

Fig. 6.1 : Competencies and Criteria for Assessment

The competencies and criteria are used for advertising the post for selection so that the potential candidates external as well as internal can self-assess their competence against the competencies and criteria. The right candidates will apply for the post. This will save the time of candidates as well as organization. The internal candidates can be provided constructive and positive feedback for improvement. The potential candidates can prepare themselves for facing the assessment process.

It is possible to set the benchmark in terms of competencies and proficiencies. For example, a Bridge engineer is to be appointed in a company working for railway. Instead of qualification and experience of candidates the company mentions about the competencies and criteria as stated in Fig 6.2. These criteria will be useful in appointing right person.

Role	Competencies	Criteria
Design all types of railway Bridge	▪ Conduct all types of survey ▪ Decide the requirements ▪ Decide the type of bridge ▪ Design the bridge ▪ Estimate the cost ▪ Prepare detail project proposal	▪ At least three surveys conducted for different types of bridges ▪ At least five bridges have been designed ▪ Used software in design of the bridge ▪ At least two proposals prepared

Fig. 6.2 : Role, Competencies, and Criteria for Bridge Engineer

The above method will reduce the processing work of selection committee at the same time the potential candidates may self-assess their performance and take decision to apply or not to apply. The selection committee can prioritize among the competencies and focus assessment on competencies, which are contributing for major share of the role. In the example given above, the core competency is design of a bridge so the candidates can be provided real life information and asked to design the railway bridge. The sound, economical, feasible, and relevant design of the bridge will be the deciding factor for selecting a candidate.

The above process can be used for redeployment of the internal professionals for a challenging or new role or assigning a new project or giving them promotion. There may be a possibility that the professional may not be adequately equipped with competencies and proficiencies to perform the role. In such a case the potential of the person is assessed against core or critical competencies related to the role.

The selection process is not so simple as it appears. In many situations the professionals are expected to perform variety of and multiple roles. They have to demonstrate variety of competencies on wide spectrum of business of organization. They are expected to be balanced in different competencies related to different roles. If we take an example of an engineering college teacher's role, it is very wide and requires variety of competencies to perform. They have to perform variety of roles and, therefore, they are required to be competent on related competencies. In such situations, the role of the teachers can be prioritized or role combinations for different teachers may be set and assessed so that right person is selected or deputed for right role. The teachers are selected in a way to perform all types of roles. The competencies can be assessed on criteria stated in Fig. 6.3. The role of teacher can be prioritized and accordingly weightage can be assigned.

Fig. 6.3 : Role, Competencies and Criteria for Selection of Teachers

Role	*Competencies*	*Criteria*
Conducting teaching learning sessions • Lectures • Discussions • Case studies • Role play • Question answers • Game • In-basket	• Conduct instructional sessions using variety of instructional methods	• Instructional plan • Instructional media • Assignments • Cases • Role description • List of questions • Presentation • Communication • Consolidation of learning • Relevance with real life
Organizing seminars, conferences, symposium	• Manage seminars, conferences, and symposium	• Plan • Database • Criteria for effectively conducting • Planning of administrative activities • Criteria for evaluation
Arranging practical sessions	• Organize laboratory experiences	• Laboratory plan • Arrangement of material • Instruction • Record maintenance
Managing projects	• Manage students projects	• Project plan • Live problem • Guidelines • Guidance and support to students • Project evaluation criteria
Managing industrial training of students	• Manage training of students	• Collaboration with industries • Training plan

Fig. 6.3 : (*Contd.*)

Role	*Competencies*	*Criteria*
		• Guidelines for training • Monitoring parameters • Problem solving mechanism • Feedback mechanism
Conducting research studies	• Conduct research studies Guide research studies	• List of emerging and new areas • Training in research • Research proposal • Research report
Conducting continuing education programmes	• Design training programmes • Conduct training programmes • Evaluate the impact of training programmes	• Training needs analysis report • Design of the programme • Instructional material • Media • Criteria for evaluation
Undertaking consultancy work	• Market the services of the institution • Prepare technical and financial proposals • Negotiate the project • Manage project	• Marketing strategy • Format of proposal • Criteria for negotiation • Training on project management
Networking with centre of excellences	• Network with centre of excellences	• Strengths and weaknesses of self and centre of excellences • Meetings and negotiations Memorandum of association
Organizing co-curricular activities	• Guide and counsel students and staff • Organize cultural activities • Organize awareness sessions and presentations of experts on various topics	• Plan for guidance and counselling • Plan for cultural activities • Plan for awareness programmes
Conducting administrative and managerial works	• Maintain records of students • Enforce discipline	• Record Management System • Records • Proof of disciplinary actions

Even in multiple roles the specific technical competency, which may be the core competency for the role, can be identified and used for selection purpose. For example, an engineering college offering Master of Technology programme in construction management should identify the core roles and competencies related to construction management for selection of the faculty and not the general qualifications and experience. In selection or placement or promotion the core competency should be given due importance.

A company is interested to appoint a counselor to harness the talent of professionals working in the company. Instead of open selection it should identify those professionals who are having wide exposure on company business and good in counseling by virtue of their interest or training, or experience or personality. The company should assess the potential of internal professionals against the counseling competencies and criteria. The company should appoint the internal candidates and train them in counseling to assume the new role. The competencies are helpful for assessing the potential at the same time assessing the performance.

3. Assessment Tools and Techniques for Selection

The assessors use variety of assessment tools and techniques for selection purpose. The assessment tools and techniques are useful to systematically gather information about the candidate on core and peripheral competencies required to perform a particular role or assume the specific position. The selection and use of right tools and techniques reduces time, efforts, and money of the assessors. In other words the validity of tools and techniques should be high for selection process. A brief description of these tools and techniques is given in subsequent paragraphs.

Profile Description

The candidates are asked to describe their significant profile against the role and competencies in terms of their qualification and experience. The role and competencies are stated in the advertisement. This technique is used for selection, promotion and redeployment purpose. The profile of different candidates can be compared and most appropriate candidates may be selected by further scrutiny. This is a screening technique commonly used where there is a possibility of receiving overwhelming response. The profile for the role is prepared as indicated in Format 6.1.

Competency Assessment

The role and a comprehensive list of competencies (core, associated, peripheral, routine, innovative etc.) is provided to the candidates and they are asked to self assess their competencies and provide justification for assessment. They are also asked to state the evidences or experiences related to each competency. The format for competency assessment is shown in Format 6.2.

Benchmarking

The benchmarking of competencies is being used in selection of professionals for challenging roles, new projects and programmes, and designing and implementing innovations. It is also used for appointing the consultant for a specific purpose. The competencies are identified on the basis of the potential roles and they are benchmarked with the professional's competencies that are already working in the organization, in the competitor's organization or world class organization and performing the similar roles. The benchmarking of competencies saves lot of time, efforts and money involved in the assessment process. It is a method of comparing the potential candidates with the best in the class.

Case Study

The human resources management department or assessors develop role related case study. The case study describes the real role demand situation in terms of data, facts, figures, problem requirement, and situation. The case study may be written as well as recorded. Recorded case study can assess the additional competencies and skills related to operation, maintenance, wastage reduction, value addition and the like. The recorded case studies are useful for every level of role because the real requirement of the role can be recorded. It is a powerful tool and technique to assess all types of competencies, i.e. cognitive, psychomotor and social. The company may develop the case studies related to the role and competencies and can be used repetitively. The company may take the help of professional case writer for developing the case study for assessment purpose. A case study to assess the competence of candidates for implementing performance appraisal system is given at the end of the chapter.

The potential candidates (internal as well as external) may be asked to analyze the case study and generate alternatives for the situation on their own. The outcome of analysis of the case study is assessed by the assessors against the competencies and criteria related to role. The candidates are selected for further assessment based on the results of the case study. The case study is used to assess the cognitive competencies such as thinking, creativity, problem solving, decision making, planning, strategy design, evaluation, and the like. The video recorded case study is useful to assess the social and attitudinal competencies such as relationship, safety, communication, concern for environment, sanitation, recognition, respect, care, and the like. It can assess lower level psychomotor competencies such as selection and use of equipment, trouble shooting, and right method of performing the task.

Role-play

Role–play is another strong technique to assess the candidates against the predefined competencies. Role-play is used in assessing the social and attitudinal competencies such as safety, cleanliness, concern for others, appreciation, pro-activeness, respect, team spirit, conservation of energy/water, positive customer relationship and the like. Social and attitudinal competencies are core competencies for some roles such as public relation, customer care, complaint handling, counseling, marketing, etc.

The assessors design a role in which the potential candidates get an opportunity to demonstrate competencies related to role. The role is explained to the potential candidates and they are asked to perform the role. While they perform the role, their behaviour is assessed on the social and attitudinal competencies. The role–play is used for assessing the potential as well as performance. The candidates consistently performing the behaviour on these roles may be considered for further scrutiny.

Presentations

Presentation is a technique used for demonstrating communication competencies. For some roles such as teachers, spokespersons, announcer, salesman, receptionist etc. the presentation is a core competency in the specific context. There could not be better method than organizing the presentations and assessing the competency on the criteria derived from the presentation competency. The presentations should be organized in simulated situation. The assessor should not get involved in contents of the presentation; otherwise they may get involved in listening and diverting from their main role of assessment. The assessors use observation schedule for assessing the quality of presentation. A sample observation schedule is given in Format 6.5.

Interview

Interviews are used as assessment tools and techniques for all types of selection, promotion, and redeployment. There are various versions of interviews as shown in Fig. 6.4.

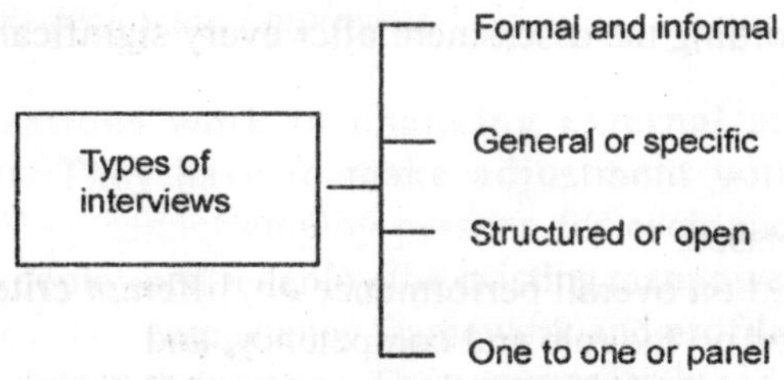

Fig. 6.4 : Types of Interviews

Each version of interview has got advantages over the others and limitations as well. Considering the need, time, availability of resource persons and budget a particular version is selected. The companies can design the tailor made interview for different positions and it may be tried out and standardized.

The assessors design assessment questions based on criteria of assessment. These questions are strong and direct measure of the competency. These questions are asked to candidates and based on the responses of candidates the assessors determine the level of competency possessed by each candidate. The assessors can also determine any extra talent related to competency. The effectiveness of interview techniques lies in interviewing skills of the assessors. They should be able to frame spontaneous probing questions to assess the depth and breadth on the competency. The assessors should observe following points for designing and conducting interview.

Interview design :

- Based on roles, competencies and criteria,
- Based on real life events,
- Consider the level of the candidates,
- Logical sequence of questions, and
- Simple to complex questions

Organizing interview :

- Supportive to candidates,
- Selection approach not rejection approach,
- Balanced with respect to time, efforts, and assessment spectrum,
- Based on ability and experience of the candidate on the required competency, and
- Recording the assessment after every significant question.

Rating :

- Unbiased,
- Based on overall performance on different criteria,
- Based on the role and competency, and
- Independent rating and not comparative rating.

In-tray Exercise

There are variety of roles that require planning, prioritization, decision-making, quick actions, strategy design, inventory management, keeping track, and the like competencies. These competencies are assessed using in-tray exercises. Role related significant exercises are designed and kept in a tray. The potential candidates are asked to clear the tray within a given time. The behaviour of the candidate is observed and assessed on well-defined criteria related to competency. The method of tray clearance and quality of decisions taken are also assessed against the well-defined criteria. In-tray exercises are used for promotion, redeployment, and fresh selection.

Problems

Problems related to core role can be selected from the real life situation and a problem bank may be prepared by the organization for assessment purpose. Role dimensions related problems might be given to potential candidates for generating alternative solutions. Based on the quality of solutions the competency of the candidates is assessed. Problems may be given in question, anecdote, and simple case study form. The routine and frequently occurred problems are selected for assessment. Problems are used in big organizations where large number of professionals are required. The organization is required to recruit, promote, and redeploy every year.

Group Discussion

Group discussion is commonly used technique in selection of professionals. It is used to assess the competencies of the candidate related to cognitive domain and working in a team. Most of the organizations of the twenty-first century are using teams' approach to achieve the challenging goals and face the competition. The group discussion is used to assess the skills related to cognitive and social competencies. An indicative list of these skills is stated in Format 6.7. The assessors use a well-designed observation schedule. They use obtrusive as well as unobtrusive observation technique depending upon the need of the situation.

Standard Tests

Standard assessment tests are also available to assess variety of competencies and skills including the personality of the potential candidates. These tests are easy to administer and take no time because electronically checked. These tests have high predictive validity. These tests are also available on testing the leadership, motivation, creativity, logic, communication, followership, interest, ambitions etc. These tests supplement the assessment process to take appropriate decisions about the candidates. If the organization is large and have full-fledged assessment centre, it should design and standardize tests. The other alternative is that the organizations having similar business should network and design a standard test for common use. The standard tests can be designed for power sector, information technology, insurance, banking, higher education, technical education, and the like. These tests should be free from culture, language, and location biases. These tests are used when the employees are redeployed for a specific assignment or role or project.

4. Criteria for Selection of Tools and Techniques

The tools and techniques of assessment are selected considering various criteria stated in Fig. 6.5.

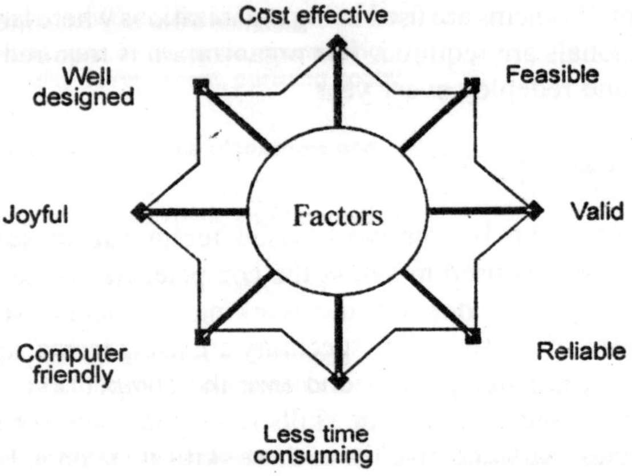

Fig. 6.5 : Criteria for Selection of Tools and Techniques

Cost Effective : The selection process should be cost effective. For internal selection, redeployment, and promotion purpose the assessment should focus on identification of full potential of the person and its full development so that the selected person may contribute for the development of the organization and get satisfaction in organizational life. The performance review of previous years is also used for assessing the potential of the person for new roles. The selection process should use the available evidences related to performance of a person in the organization. The past performance should not only be the base for assessment for new role. In some situations it may mislead about the potential of the person. For example, a professor has not been provided an opportunity to do research work in last five years so her/his achievements on research is nil. It does not mean that the professor is not having the potential to do research work. The assessment, appraisal, and evaluation in the organization should be systematically recorded to reduce the assessment cost for future placement, development, and training.

Feasible : The assessment tools and techniques should be so selected that they are familiar to assessor, assessees, and organization. It should not require complete design and training to use them.

Otherwise the preparation for assessment process will take longer time than carrying out the assessment process. It will consume more time and money as well. The tools should be easy to administer, check and interpret. It should not require much of expertise or additional expertise, which is not available with the organization.

Valid : The tools and techniques should measure the competencies against the potential role. They should measure on the whole spectrum of the role and not on one or two dimensions of the role. The tools and techniques not only measure the current competencies but potential for developing related competencies in near future. If the organization is in a business, which is of changing nature than the competencies related to adapting, adopting, adjusting, and collaborating should also be assessed in candidates.

Reliable : The tools and techniques should be reliable so that they consistently measure the competence of the potential candidates. To enhance the validity and reliability of the tools and techniques the organization should pilot the tools and techniques before large-scale use. If the organization is selecting tools and techniques designed by sister organization it should modify them according to requirements of the role.

Less Time Consuming : The tools and techniques are selected in such a way so that they take minimum time. For this purpose the assessors should use computer friendly tools and techniques. The strong and direct indicators should be used in the assessment tools. Tools and techniques in which the candidate involvement is more and involvement of the experts is less should be used. The preliminary scrutiny of the candidates should be carried out on the basis of resumé and portfolio submitted by them. The advertisement should be designed to encourage deserving candidates to apply and discourage casually applying candidates.

Computer Friendly : The cognitive competencies and knowledge part of the social and psychomotor competencies should be assessed using standard tests designed for the purpose. The answer sheet should be electronically checked to save the time, efforts and money. The computer simulation and game may be used to assess the higher level cognitive and lower level psychomotor competencies.

Joyful : The assessment tools and techniques should create sense of achievement and joy. They should create interest to attempt the items and questions. The tools and techniques should create enough challenge for the potential candidates. The potential candidates should be attracted to get the job on the basis of the assessment tools and techniques. The process should not create any tension or stress. The process should not waste the time of the candidates. The interaction with senior officials, visit of the work place, understanding the challenges of the role at work place are some methods that facilitates assessment at the same time create excitement for the job.

Well Designed : The tools and techniques should be scientifically designed using principles of assessment, learning, and education technology. The process should be simple, logical, and clear to the candidates. A flow chart or tree diagram can be used for designing the assessment process. It should be complete and assess all the dimensions of role in one go. The organization should deploy adequate resources to minimize the wastage of time of candidates. The candidates should be acquainted with the assessment procedure before entering in it.

5. Issues in Assessment for Selection

In competency based assessment process and for that matter in other selection processes, there are number of issues that needs to be considered and addressed appropriately. These issues are stated below :

Selection against

1. Present competencies or future competencies.
2. Past performance or aspirations.
3. Core competence or professional competence.
4. Routine competencies or non-routine competencies.
5. On the basis of references or rigorous competency assessment.
6. Under competence or over competence.
7. Known person or unknown person.
8. Performance record or potential to perform.

6. Summary

Recruitment of right person for the organization is necessary for ensuring growth and development of the organization. The right person for right job will perform effectively, efficiently, and professionally to bring variety of benefits to the organization. On the contrary wrong selection of the person for the right job may become the liability to the organization and fellow members. The organizations should use competency approach to select the persons for a particular role. The competencies are derived from the present and near future role requirement in the organization. Based on the role related competencies the selection process can be designed. The competencies requirement varies from role to role. For one type of role the major competencies may fall in cognitive domain and for other type of role they may fall in affective/social domain. There are number of tools and techniques used for selecting a person for a particular role. These tools and techniques are selected considering their strengths and limitations. The tools and techniques such as candidate profile, competency assessment, benchmarking, case study, role-play, presentations, interviews, in-tray exercises, problems, group discussions and standard tests are designed and used. The tools and techniques are selected using various criteria such as cost effectiveness, feasibility, validity, reliability, less time consuming, computer friendly, joyful and well designed.

7. Format

Format 6.1 : *Profile Description*

The profile is derived from the role to be assumed by the person. The role profile of the project manager for rural development project is given in the Format 6.1.

Project leader at district level

Sl. No.	*Profile*	*Achievement*	*Rating*
1.	*Qualification* Master of social works with specialization in watershed management		
2.	Completed three medium watershed projects (500 hectares each) as a team leader in past three years		
3.	Trained in participatory rural appraisal for two weeks in last three years		
4.	Trained in watershed management project design using logical framework approach		
5.	Prepared at least one project proposal using participatory approach and logical framework model		

Format 6.1 : (Contd.)

Sl. No.	Profile	Achievement	Rating
6.	Prepared at least one project completion report on watershed project management		
7.	Worked on at least one project in tribal area		
8.	Published at least one paper on project management experiences		
9.	Ready to work in interior district of the State		
10.	Willing to receive training on project management		

Format 6.2* : *Competency Assessment

Role: Corporate leadership
Legend: 4–Very High, 3–High, 2–Low, 1–Very Low

Sl. No.	Competencies	Self-assessment	Evidences
A.	Core		
▪	Provide vision to organization		
▪	Initiate change and innovation		
▪	Enhance corporate reputation of the organization		
▪	Market the product and services		
▪	Network and collaborate for mutual benefit		
B.	Associated		
▪	Promote teams structure		
▪	Assure quality in products and services		
▪	Minimize waste		
▪	Increase employee satisfaction		
▪	Use information technology		
C.	Innovative		
▪	Explore unknown business venture		
▪	Use aggressive strategy		

Format 6.3*: *Case Study

A big industry and education group having more than 30 engineering and higher education institution is interested to appoint the performance appraisal experts to modify the performance appraisal system to suit the current and future requirements of the institutions. It wants to appoint 15 experts. The assessors use following case study for assessing the expertise of the experts.

S.Z. Polytechnic is an autonomous polytechnic. It is a 40 years old polytechnic. This Polytechnic offers 10 diploma and 5 post-diploma programmes in conventional and hi-tech disciplines including information technology. The Polytechnic has received huge resources from Central and State Governments for modernization and updating the facilities from time to time. It was also considered under Strengthening Technician Education Project assisted by World Bank. Prof. B.L. Gupta has recently taken over the charge of the Principal. He is surprised to see the huge resources lying underutilized including the human resources. Prof. Gupta is trained in education management and he knows various management techniques to increase the utilization of resources. He believes in harnessing the potential of human resources. He thinks that if human resources are utilized properly, utilization of other resources will improve automatically. Prof. Gupta has attended training programme of one week duration in Technical Teachers' Training Institute, on enhancing faculty contribution. Prof. Shivagunde was the coordinator of the programme. Prof. Shivagunde preached that there are number of factors, which can be redesigned for encouraging faculty members to excel better. Some of the factors he preached are listed below :

- Challenging work,
- Interesting work,
- Variety of work,
- Freedom for action,
- Responsibility,
- Sense of accomplishment,
- Opportunity for personal growth and development,
- Recognition of achievements,
- Friendly atmosphere and good working conditions,
- Vision for the future, and
- Dynamic and shared leadership etc.

Prof. Shivagunde had also promoted the concept that plans should be prepared at institutional, departmental and individual level. Plans so prepared should be clear, specific, realistic, and flexible. He had promoted the concept of 'Performance Appraisal' during the training programme. He preached that performance appraisal system should be well designed and introduced in the institution. It should be open, participative, data based, objective, transparent, and flexible.

Each teacher should prepare individual plan at the beginning of the academic year. This plan should be in tune with the departmental and institutional plan. This idea clicked to Prof. B.L. Gupta, Principal of the institute and he decided to implement the performance appraisal system in his institute along with other good factors. He called a meeting of head of departments and briefed them about the training programme he attended and shown his determination to introduce the performance appraisal system in the institution.

He asked three head of departments of conventional discipline to revise the format of confidential report system. Three head of departments, who are experienced people, designed one format applicable to all levels of faculty and staff members. This format is a little bit modified version of the confidential report system format. They placed the format for approval before the principal. Principal Gupta was busy at that moment of time and was under pressure for organizing society meeting so with minor modification he approved the format and asked three head of departments to get it printed and distribute to all the faculty and staff members. They did so.

One head of department out of three in the committee called all the faculty and staff members of his department. He fired them commenting about their unsatisfactory performance. He warned them and asked them to improve performance in left out period of the year. At the end of the year he appraised the performance of all the faculty and staff members. He assigned fair and good to all the faculty and staff members on all the dimensions of the format and asked them to improve upon the performance otherwise he will not tolerate it next year.

Two other heads of departments have assigned very good to most of the faculty and staff members with few exceptions of good and excellent. Other heads of departments did not take much interest in introducing the performance appraisal. They simply graded the performance as they used to do in the past. One head of department called a lecturer Mr. Asati and commented on his performance that he performed excellent but is being awarded good. If he continues to perform excellent next year also then he can be graded excellent. Some of the staff members were shirkers so most of the head of departments graded them fair or good. But one head of department issued show cause notice to one staff member for poor performance.

As Principal Gupta received the appraisal report of faculty and staff members well in time but at the same time he received many complaints about head of departments. Some complaints were related to misappropriation of funds and misbehaviour. All the faculty and staff members were against the new system of performance appraisal. They met the Principal with the request to continue the previous system. They also threatened the Principal indicating that if their request is not accepted they will go on strike.

Issues for Discussion

Q1. Was Principal's strategy to implement performance appraisal system okay ?
   (a) If yes, highlight the strengths of the strategy.
   (b) If no, state what are the weaknesses ?

Q2. Design suitable alternative strategies to implement performance appraisal system in S.Z. Polytechnic.

Format 6.4: *Role Play*

A cell phone company is interested to appoint customer care manager in its head office. The customer care manager is expected to handle complaints received telephonically. The potential candidate has to perform the role of complaint handling for 15 minutes receiving complaints on phone. The behaviour of the candidate is observed on different criteria using observation sheet.

Observation of Candidate's Behaviour on Customer Care

Legend: 5—Excellent, 4—Very Good, 3—Good, 2—Poor, 1—Very Poor

Behaviour	*Quality of demonstration*
Greeting	
Listening skills	
Clarifying the complaint	
Understanding the extent of complaint	
Recording the complaint	
Responding to the complainer	
Classifying the complaint	
Communicating the complaint to the relevant section	
Ensuring the complaint removal	
Informing the complainant	

Format 6.5: Assessment of Presentation Competency

The presentation competency of the candidate for selection purpose can be assessed on the indicative criteria stated in the table given below:

Assessment of Presentation Competency of Candidate

Legend **: 5—Excellent, 4—Very Good, 3—Good, 2—Poor, 1—Very Poor**

Sl. No.	*Behaviour*	*Quality of demonstration*
▪	Greeting	
▪	Advance information on presentation	
▪	Logic and sequence in presentation	
▪	Richness in subject matter	
▪	Comprehensiveness	
▪	New and different information	
▪	Use of incidences and anecdotes	
▪	Command on language	
▪	Quality of voice	
▪	Quality of appropriateness of body language	
▪	Effectiveness of preparation and use of media	
▪	Change of stimulus during presentation	
▪	Involvement of audience	
▪	Quality of attraction of audience	
▪	Time management	
▪	Reinforcement of key message	
▪	Quality of handling the questions of audience	
▪	Effectiveness of influencing the audience	
▪	Level of confidence throughout the presentation	
▪	Quality of closing the presentation	

Format 6.6 : Interview

Interview for principal of private engineering college

Questions	*Response*
How will you craft the vision of the institution?	
How will you influence the faculty and staff members to achieve the crafted vision?	
How will you achieve excellence in teaching learning, research and consultancy?	

Format 6.6 : (*Contd.*)

Questions	*Response*
What type of autonomy do you require to enhance the corporate reputation of the institution?	
Which methods will you use to harness the full potential of students for their career?	
How much time do you need to significantly improve the results of the students in university examination?	
Which immediate actions will you take to improve the results of students?	

Format 6.7* : *Assessment of Competencies through Group Discussion

The cognitive and working in a team skills of the candidate for selection purpose can be assessed on the indicative criteria stated in the table given below.

Assessment of cognitive and team skills of candidate

Legend: 5—Excellent, 4—Very Good, 3—Good, 2—Poor, 1—Very poor

Behaviour	*Quality of demonstration*
Rapport building	
Motivating	
Deciding the issue	
Influencing	
Communicating	
Convincing	
Setting the challenging goals	
Harnessing creativity of the group	
Consensus seeking	
Arguing	
Negotiating	
Decision making	
Listening	
Obtaining commitment	
Making presentation	
Resolving conflict	
Accepting challenge	
Creating challenge	
Rewarding	

8. Review Questions

1. State the need and importance of assessment for recruitment.
2. Define competency-based assessment for recruitment.
3. Explain the process for deriving competencies for recruitment.
4. State the assessment tools and techniques used for recruitment and selection.
5. Explain the profile description method of assessment.
6. Explain the advantages and limitations of competency assessment method.
7. List the benefits of benchmarking of competencies in assessment for recruitment.
8. Describe the method of using case study for assessment.
9. List the competencies/skills that can be assessed using role-play method.
10. Explain the advantages of using presentation. Which competencies are predominantly assessed using presentation?
11. Describe the process of conducting interview for redeployment of the professionals.
12. State the competencies/skills assessed using in-tray exercises.
13. List the basic purpose of problem solving exercises in assessment for selection.
14. State the competencies/skills used in group discussion method.
15. List the advantages of using standard tests over other methods of assessment.
16. State the criteria for selection of methods.
17. Compare the tools and techniques of assessment used for assessing cognitive competencies.

9. Activities for HR Managers

Activity 6.1: Selection of Public Relation Officer

Design assessment tool for assessing candidates for appointment on the post of Public Relation Officer for an engineering college. The basic role of the person will be related to marketing the services of the institution to stakeholders.

Activity 6.2: Selection of Receptionist

Design interview schedule for selecting a receptionist in the corporate office of an automobile dealer's organization.

Activity 6.3: Selection of Customer Care Officer

Design an instrument to select Customer Care Officer in Cell Phone Company.

Activity 6.4: Selection of Turner

Design an instrument to select a Turner for gear manufacturing company.

7

Competency Based Training

LEARNING OBJECTIVES

After reading this chapter the readers will be able to :

1. State the need and importance of training.
2. Define the concept of training in changing context.
3. State the benefits of professional training.
4. Describe the characteristics of training.
5. Explain the training management model.
6. List the significant stakeholders involved in management of training.
7. Describe the stake of stakeholders in management of training.
8. Explain the importance of competency based training programmes.
9. State the classification of competencies.
10. Describe the purpose of competency based training programmes.
11. List the characteristics of competency based training programmes.
12. Explain the shift required in training in twenty-first century.

1. Introduction

The competencies are developed and refined using various approaches such as training, education, guidance, counseling, mentoring, coaching self learning, and gaining experiences. All these approaches are used by organizations to bring the level of individuals and teams up to expected level so that they perform effectively and efficiently.

The market has become dynamic and turbulent. Every organization is continuously changing and updating itself to stay in the market place. The globalization of economic, technological, social, cultural and educational dimensions has significantly affected the functioning of corporate sector and even government sector. The companies are diversifying, changing, merging, expanding, collaborating, networking, and withdrawing from the market place to cope up with the environment.

The corporate sector is investing crores of rupees in tuning its business to suit the demand of the market. It is pouring money in terms of technology, techniques, manpower, research, marketing and so on. It is obvious that the corporate sector would prefer and employ competent, proficient and entrepreneurs in their business. There is a great change and shift in the role of the professionals. This requires continuous refinement, updating and learning new technical and professional competencies.

The fast development of concepts, knowledge, principles and philosophy in the field of management is facilitating the changing business of organization at the same time it is creating the opportunities for training and development of the professional. In the past two decades, number of models and philosophies evolved for management of the organization. In fact, it was the practice and experimentation of many organizations that contributed to management philosophies.

The philosophy of management by objectives was the turning point and it laid the foundation for emergence of other philosophies and theories. To name a few Total quality management, Kizen, Just in time, Business process reengineering, Zero defect, Continuous improvement, Capacity maturity model, Visioning, Enterprise resources planning, Logical framework, Teams structure, Organization excellence, Learning organization, Six sigma, 360 degree feedback, etc. have changed the method of doing the business. This calls for continuous training of professionals and employees.

The concept of value addition in the corporate world need to be considered in training sector to enable the professionals to stay competent, proficient, effective, efficient and satisfying in changing environment. The concept of value addition in training should be seen from many dimensions such as technical, entrepreneurial, managerial, research, social, linguistic, coping, change management, learning, thinking, and emotional intelligence and so on. The value addition needs to be considered from enhancing proficiency level in core competencies. It can be seen from reducing the time, cost and stress of learning. It can be seen from increasing joy and interest in learning and achieving self actualization level, pursuing hobby, career and so on.

2. Concept of Training

The concept of training has a greater and wider scope. It is defined in relation to organization and its business. However, it is an opportunity created by the organization for its employees to develop themselves to self-actualization level in order to harness and use their full potential for the development of the organization and derive satisfaction out of it. They personally feel proud of being part of the organization and project corporate image of the organization to expand the business to earn profit.

The concept of training has evolved over the years along with evolution of business. It focuses on empowering the professionals for learning and developing their competence and proficiency to highest level. It focuses on renewal of learning and developing new and different competencies as per requirements of the business. The whole concept of training has shifted to create every person in the organization as a trainer of self and others. The training is considered as a part of the business strategy and as an investment. The training focuses on learning and developing competence and proficiency for accepting the challenges and meeting the competitions.

The boundaries of training have crossed human resources development department and spread all over the organization. Training is considered the business of every professional and employee of the organization. Training is a continuous process in the organization. It is imparted formally and informally to empower people to perform proficiently. The opportunity for learning is created in the organization and outside the organization. The whole purpose of the training is to make the organization proactive and responsive to changing environment in contrast to traditional reactive approach of training. The organization considers every opportunity as learning opportunity.

3. Benefits of Training

The benefits of competency based training are many and vivid. It ranges from micro level to meta level. The benefits are derived from training needs and training cycle. The benefits are shown in Fig. 7.1.

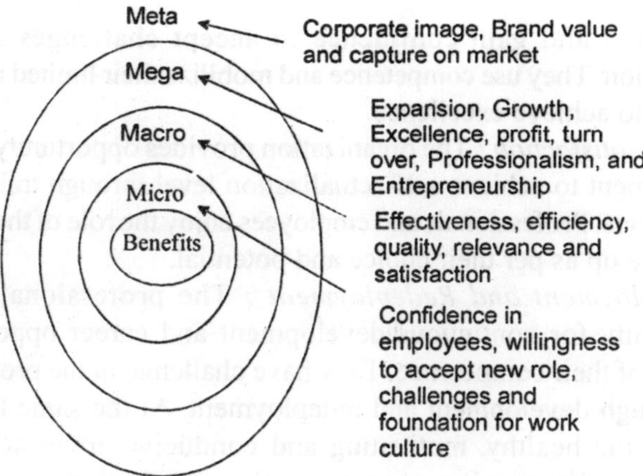

Fig. 7.1 : Benefits of Competency Based Training

Training has direct and indirect impact on the performance, growth and development of the organization at the same time it enables the professionals to satisfy and delight the customers. The significant benefits of the training are listed in following paragraphs.

Development of Core Competence : Training helps to develop the competency and proficiency of the professionals and employees to perform professionally even in changing situation. The organization assures the quality of the business on the basis of core competence of its employees.

Assure Productivity and Quality : Trained professionals utilize full capacity of machines and materials for higher productivity and profit. There is no scope for waste of money, time and efforts of people thereby cutting down the cost of the product and services. At the same time quality of the product and services are assured to satisfy the needs of the customers. They observe safety habits thereby preventing and reducing accidents and controlling pollution.

Promote Corporate Culture : Trained professionals work in teams and in a cooperative manner. They foster creativity and innovation and prevent conflicts and problems. They adhere to values, norms, ethics and beliefs of the organization in order to work cohesively in a joyful way. The change can be implemented in a natural way without resistance for change.

Progress Towards Excellence and Vision : They predict the barriers, obstacles, hurdles and problems of journey to vision. They prepare themselves and gain confidence to accept challenges and face competition. They use competence and mobilize their limited resources in order to achieve excellence.

Self-satisfaction : The organization provides opportunity for self-development to achieve self-actualization level through training and other means. Professionals and employees enjoy the role of their choice and move up as per their choice and potential.

Deployment and Redeployment : The professionals get an opportunity for continuous development and career opportunities because of their competence. They have challenge in the professional life through development and redeployment. At the same time they work in the healthy, motivating and conducive environment that enhances their commitment to stay in the organization.

Base for Continual Training and Learning : Well designed training programmes provide continuity in learning process. The professionals sustain their professionalism in changing environment and changing role. They are never outdated. They flow and perform with the changing needs of the business.

Incentive : Training is considered as incentive by professionals. They learn on the expenses of the organization. They learn to explore better opportunities for them within the organization and outside the organization. They receive incentives after successful completion of training.

Training is not considered panacea for organizational problems. It cannot substitute the physical resources and financial resources. It cannot overcome the market recession and other organizational limitations. It will not work in organizations where hygiene factors are poorly existent and motivational factors are absent.

4. Characteristics of Training

Professionally planned, designed, implemented and assessed training is considered investment. It enhances organizational performance and brings positive impact on the business of the organization. It improves the method of doing the business. The professionally offered training has characteristics stated below :

Part of Business : Training is considered as a part of the business of the organization. The design of the training goes with the design of the business. Training complement and supplement the business of the organization. It is managed as professionally as the business of the organization.

Continuous Process : Training is a process and it is offered continuously in the organization and outside the organization. It is linear process in contrast to cyclic that is commonly practiced. In training process approach is used to assure and ensure competency and proficiency development of professionals in contrast to blue print approach.

Holistic Approach : It is planned in totality for the whole business of the organization. The training focuses on future business of the organization rather than solving problems, resolving crisis, or improving performance of an individual or a section. The decisions are made considering all the professionals and employees.

Customer Focus : The training is designed considering the expectations of the customers. The training is planned to reply the question, how will it contribute to customer satisfaction? The training contributes for improving the performance of the whole organization.

Enhance Professionalism : The training enhances the professional approach of employees. It increases productivity, reduce wastage, improve quality, promote healthy climate, increase professional satisfaction etc.

Participative : Participative training approaches are used to enhance commitment of employees and identify their specific needs. The talent, creativity, experiences and performance problems of employees are shared in the training programmes.

Build Capacity : The training builds capacity in the organization and buffer of expertise and experience to deal with any external and internal situation for sustenance, growth, development and expansion.

5. Training Management Model

The training brings impact on the performance of the organization. At the same time it is effective, efficient, relevant and purposeful. The training is managed professionally in the organization. A systematic approach to training is used by organizations to satisfy the training needs of the employees. The model shown in Fig. 7.2 describes the various phases of training, their definitions, purpose, techniques, tools, and output.

Fig. 7.2 : Systematic Approach to Training

Parameters	*Needs analysis*	*Design*	*Implementation*	*Evaluation*
Definition	It is a systematic and scientific method of identifying the present and near future needs of the customers and stakeholders and translating them into roles of employees. These roles are classified, prioritized and competencies of employees are derived.	It is a systematic and scientific method of translating the validated roles of employees in the form of competencies, competency maps, and designing learning processes to develop competency.	It is a systematic and scientific method of preparing and implementing training plans, organizing learning and other necessary resources in order to develop stated competency in employees and assessing them for certification.	It is a systematic and scientific method of drawing conclusions about effectiveness and efficiency of training programmes and assessing the impact of it on the business of the organization and satisfaction of employees.
Purpose	To identify the expectations of customers and stakeholders and provide sound foundation for designing, implementing and evaluating the training. At the same time making the training relevant, effective, efficient, and need based.	To provide a well design plan to develop professional competence in employees and commit resources to training. To develop learning resources and decide learning and assessment methods.	To translate provisions of training in reality assuring quality, relevance, effectiveness, and efficiency in implementation of learning process.	To draw conclusions about effectivenes, efficiency, relevance, quality, strengths, gaps, and weaknesses in training. To explore opportunities for improvement and value addition.
Methods	Study of technology and techniques used in	Assessing the current level of competence and identifying	Policy to implement competency based training	Decide the purpose of evaluation Evaluation of

Fig. 7.2 : (*Contd.*)

Parameters	*Needs analysis*	*Design*	*Implementation*	*Evaluation*
	organization, methods of working, work culture, legal provisions, competition, challenges, roles analysis, career progression, expectations of significant stakeholders, future plans, problems, future technology, and opportunities.	the gaps, Preparing training plan Designing learning processes, learning resources, learning methods, assessment methods to develop competency. Organizing physical and learning resources.	programmes Creation of essential facilities Implementing training plan Assessment of training output Records management Certification of competency.	whole training cycle or specific phase, Decide evaluation parameters such as improvement in production, quality, and profit Reduction in problems, waste, breakdown, conflicts, litigations etc.
Techniques	Snap study, search conference, interview, focus group discussions, document analysis, meetings, SWOT analysis, Creativity techniques such as Delphi, Nominal group technique, Brain storming, Cognitive mapping Literature search of future industry trends.	Bench marking, prioritization, Creativity techniques such as Delphi, Nominal group technique, Brain storming, Cognitive mapping.	Assessing entry behaviour of the trainees Learning methods Learning resources Physical resources.	Evaluation tools such as purpose of evaluations, criteria for evaluation, research instruments Management survey, peer survey, record of output and innovations.
Tools	Interview schedule Questionnaire Issues for discussion Criteria for	Cognitive mapping Content analysis Literature search	Learning resources Learning methods Assessment methods	Tracer study Impact study

Fig. 7.2 : (*Contd.*)

Parameters	*Needs analysis*	*Design*	*Implementation*	*Evaluation*
	analysis. Rating scale. Observation. form. SWOT. Performance standards	Competency map Process design Skills analysis	Training plans Training implementation plans	
Outputs	Needs of industry and stakeholders Training needs in the form of competencies and competencies gap with reference to present and future	Training plans Implementation guide Assessment guide Bròchure for stakeholders	Competent and professional employees ready to work	Report on refining, revising, reengineering the whole training plan or particular phases, implementa-tion and assessment
Responsibility	Training design team	Training design team	Training centres/ institution and organization	Training design/evalu-ation team

6. Stakeholders in Training Management

There are numerous stakeholders to training programmes. Stakeholders are those individuals, groups and organizations who can affect the training programmes of the organization in positive or negative way. The effectiveness and efficiency of the business of the organization depends on these stakeholders. Stakeholders also depend on the organization to do their business successfully.

The management of the stakeholders is one of the important and significant activities of the organization. The organization should identify the significant stakeholders and group them according to their interest, choice and extent of stake. Some stakeholders may be significant during the planning phase, some may be during the design, some may be during the implementation phase and some may be during the evaluation phase. Some stakeholders may be significant throughout the life cycle of the training programme. The stakeholders may be different for different training programmes of the organization.

The organization can classify the stakeholders according to phases of life cycle of training programmes. The organization designs strategies to manage the stakeholders to get their favour, support, guidance and facilities for conducting the training programmes. It should share expertise, experiences and resources to design and implement the training programmes. It should collaborate, cooperate and network with them for academic benefits. At the same time there is need to manage the stakeholders who are negative, unfavourable and in competition. The negative stakeholders can be very well managed using professional approaches and hitting their weaknesses. The organization creates a collaborative situation to manage the negative stakeholders. An indicative list of significant stakeholders is shown in Fig. 7.3.

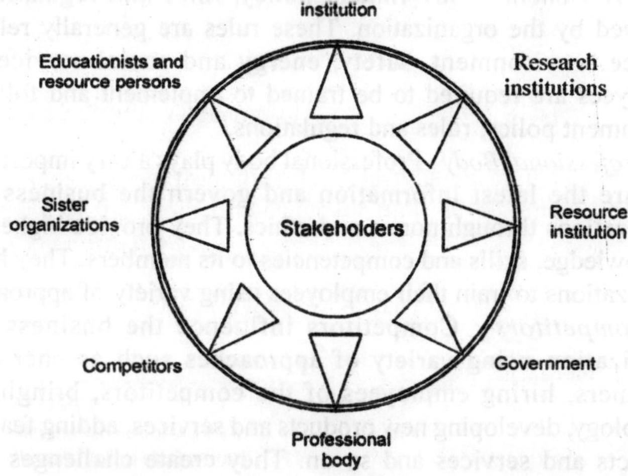

Fig 7.3 : Stakeholders of Training Programmes

Training Institutions : Training institutions play a significant role in designing and implementing the training programmes. Selection of professional training institutions for imparting training is a sort of motivation for the trainees to receive the training. The training imparted by professional training institutions brings improvement in the performance of the organization.

Research Institutions : Research institutions contribute new and efficient technology to carry out the business of the organization. The selection of right technology and techniques at right time put the organization in leading position in the market. The introduction of new technology requires training of employees. The new technology and techniques saves time, efforts and money and enhances product quality and production efficiency.

Resource Institutions : There are number of government and private organizations having resources and know how to expand and develop business. These institutions undertake consultancy work and carry out the projects on behalf of the organization. These institutions handover the project and impart training to organizational members to operate the project and carry out the business or implement the innovations. One time activity should be assigned to resource organization.

Government : Government policy, rules and regulations are observed by the organization. These rules are generally related to finance, environment, safety, energy and social services. The employees are required to be trained to implement and follow the government policy, rules and regulations.

Professional Body : Professional body plays a very important role to share the latest information and govern the business of the organizations through norms and ethics. They provide highest level of knowledge, skills and competencies to its members. They help the organizations to train their employees using variety of approaches.

Competitors : Competitors influence the business of the organization using variety of approaches such as encroaching customers, hiring employees of the competitors, bringing new technology, developing new products and services, adding features to products and services and so on. They create challenges for the organizations to cope up with them. The competition is successfully faced by organization through training.

Sister Organizations : They implement change and innovations with a specific purpose. They train their employees and set a benchmark in training for others to follow. Observing the practices in sister organizations people plan training interventions in their organizations.

Educationists and Resource Persons: They are the prime mover of the systematic and scientific training programmes. On the one hand educationists help in designing and conducting the training programmes and on the other hand the resource persons facilitate the training providing latest learning inputs in their disciplines.

7. Competency Based Training Programmes

Competency-based training is a plan to develop professionally competent and proficient employees to assume responsibility, accept and face challenges of the corporate world and enjoy professional life. The competencies are identified and classified through training needs analysis. The classification of competencies depends on the type of the organization and its business. In construction engineering working safety may be peripheral or associative competency but in chemical engineering or mechanical engineering it can be core competency.

The new disciplines are emerging in fast changing world. There should be provisions in the training programmes or career planning to shift from one discipline to another over a period of time achieving core or essential competencies through training and formal or informal education programmes of universities.

The organization prepares competency maps for each category of professionals and employees establishing vertical, horizontal and diagonal logic. It indicates broad learning strategies to achieve the stated learning outcomes and resources required to implement the learning strategies. It spells out the significant learning processes that are to be carried out in order to implement the strategy and achieve the learning outcomes.

The learning processes include learning resources, learning experiences and learning opportunities. This is the base plan for which rest of the supporting plans, processes and activities are performed in the training centre/institution to supplement and complement the training implementation strategy. The assessment scheme and method of certification of competency is described in the training plan. The method of evaluation of the training plan and impact of assessment of the competency-based training is also described in the training plan.

8. Need and Importance of Competency Based Training Programmes

The roles of the employees become the base for designing training programmes. These roles are translated in the form of learning output produced through training programmes. These learning outputs are spelled out in specific, measurable, attainable, realistic, and time bound statements. These learning outputs are expressed in terms of competency and proficiency. The process of translating the expectations of the stakeholders in terms of roles and competencies of professional programme is shown in Fig. 7.4.

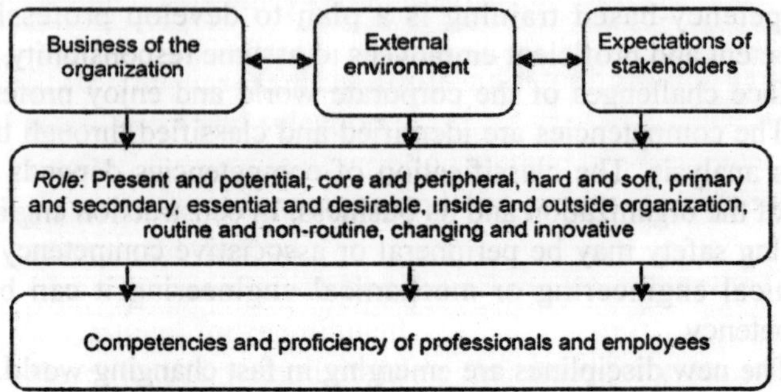

Fig. 7.4 : Derivation of Competencies

Having decided the output of educational and training programmes in terms of competencies the training plans are designed scientifically to produce professionals to take up the new and changing positions in the organization. The need and importance of competency based training programmes are briefly described below :

Objectivity : It provides the objectivity in offering training to professionals and employees to cater the human resources requirements of the organization. It encompasses the roles, aims and competencies that are helpful to prepare detailed training plans of the organization.

Tool of Communication : It is a strong communication tool for communicating with external and internal stakeholders of the organization on various dimensions of training and development.

Unity of Actions : It provides unity of actions among various departments, sections and teams of the organization. It becomes the base to derive roles of training team/training division and accordingly prepare them to take up the role.

Alignment of Actions : The training plans precisely spell out the roles, aims and competencies to be developed in professionals and employees. So the training processes and actions are appropriately designed and aligned in order to achieve the competencies. The redundant actions and activities related to training and development are dropped down to save time, money and energy.

Organization of Resources : The organization organizes all necessary resources on the basis of training plans. Adequate budget is allocated for training. At the same time the trainees are sponsored for training in a planned way so that the production/services/organizational activities do not suffer.

Human Resources Development: The competency-based training becomes the base for developing the professionals and employees in order to implement the training cycle effectively and efficiently. They are developed to become the resource person for imparting training to organizational members. The competent employees will not make mistakes thereby reducing the cost of production.

Marketing Products and Services of the Organization : The products and services of the organization are professionally developed by trained persons assuring the quality fulfilling the international requirements so it is easy to market the products and services at higher value.

Comparability: The international organizations are using competency-based approach in training. The training can be compared with other organizations for various purposes such as benchmarking, allocating the budget, defining the proficiency of the professionals etc.

Universal Acceptability : Competency based training is universally acceptable. It is easy to get recognition of capability and capacity of professionals. It helps the organizations to collaborate, network, and merge with international organizations.

Valid and Reliable Certification : The objectivity in measurement of learning outcomes and level of proficiency in competency is helpful to award authentic certificate on competency profile and proficiency level.

Establishing Equivalence : The competencies are recognized all over the world so recognition of prior learning can be given anywhere in the world. Further education can be planned at any time in the professional life as per requirement.

Flexibility in Achieving Competencies : Competencies and cluster of competencies can be grouped to perform a particular role. The competencies/group of competencies can be achieved at any time, duration, and place.

9. Purpose of Competency Based Training

The purpose of competency-based training is wide and broad. It is not limited to boundaries of the organization. It addresses the expectations of all the significant stakeholders. It is a plan for offering education and training to employees to make them capable to take up developmental activities of the organization including accomplishing the vision.

The competency based training plan is an important document that is useful to everyone inside and outside the organization. The one significant strength of competency-based training programmes is that it assures the development of professionals. The competency-based training plans fulfil the needs and serves variety of purposes. Some of the indicative purposes are stated below :

- Base for communication on training programmes with internal and external stakeholders for various purposes.
- Unity in action is maintained among training implementers.
- Provide sense of order and direction for implementation.
- Ensure cooperation, commitment and support from various stakeholders.
- The monitoring of the progress on training is objective and implementation problems can be detected at early stage.
- The resources can be deployed at right time to minimize wastage.
- Implementation crisis can be prevented and minimized.
- Quality of training and learning can be assured.
- Learning challenges can be designed and implemented.
- Valid and reliable assessment system can be implemented.
- Flexibility in learning can be offered.
- Feedback on quality of training can be obtained from stakeholders to timely revise, modify, refine and re-engineer training plan.
- Marketing of the products and services of the organization.
- Remove the perception, biases and subjectivity in training management.
- Guide to focus on training processes.
- Commitment of individuals and teams for implementation.
- Role clarity of implementers.
- Help to take effective decisions.
- Lead to feeling of success.
- Reveal future opportunities.
- Base for getting accreditation of the training programmes and business of the organization from national and international certifying agencies.
- Instrument for collaborating, networking and expanding the business area of the organization.

10. Characteristics of Competency Based Training Programmes

The competency based training programmes are different than other content based programmes. It is distinct and unique from other training programmes in many ways as it is clear from following characteristics:

Professionally Designed: It is professionally designed using scientific methods of training design by a team of experts from various disciplines such as technologist, engineering educationalist, industry expert, psychologist/andragogist, expert trainers and so on.

Logically Driven: The training plans describe the roles that are performed and need to be performed by employees. It addresses the need of multiple, variety of, and shifting roles. It states the competencies to perform the roles in corporate world. The competencies are classified according to the requirements of the role and position. The classification of competencies is carried out under different heads such as technical, managerial, entrepreneurial, social, research, change management and so on. The other methods of classifying the competencies are based on role such as present and potential, core and peripheral, hard and soft, primary and secondary, essential and desirable, inside and outside organization, routine and non-routine, changing and innovative.

The competency map indicating the logic in attaining the competencies is prepared. The vertical, horizontal and diagonal link between competencies is indicated in the competency map. The proficiency level in each competency is defined as per prevailing and expected proficiency level in the organization. It indicates the competency relation diagram to move from elementary to advance, simple to complex and concrete to abstract competencies. The competency relationship diagram provides the flexibility to achieve the competencies.

Research Based : The competency based training plan is based on research. It is not based of hunches, opinions and views of few persons as practiced in many organizations. It is data based.

Focus on Present as well as Future : It focuses on development of present as well as future competencies. The competencies are developed to achieve missions and vision of the organization.

Entry Behaviour of the Employees : It matches with different entry behaviours of employees on various aspects such as social, cultural, technical, general intelligence, learning attitude, ambition and so on. It suggests the prerequisite qualifications or competency if any to develop advance competencies.

Focus on Core Competence : It gives more emphasis on defining and developing core competencies. The peripheral, associative and supportive competencies are an integral part and by-product of learning process.

Bench Marked : The whole training plan is bench marked with the best in the world to enable the employees comparable with the best.

No Wastage : The training plan ensures that there is no repetition of learning events to minimize wastage of time, efforts and money.

Flexible Behaviour : It develops behaviour to adjust, adopt, adapt in diverse work culture, society, teams, and geographic areas.

Flexibility: It incorporates adequate flexibility in approach, time, and learning style. It defines alternative approaches to achieve competency and time frame to achieve the same. It suggests alternative learning methods to be used to attain the competency effectively and efficiently.

Self-explanatory : The technical terms are well defined in the training plan to make it self-explanatory to implementers.

Scope for Creativity and Innovation : The training plan creates enough scope for using individual, group and trainer creativity to develop creative and innovative competencies.

Emphasize on self-learning : The training plans incorporate concepts of learning to learn, thinking, and learning for life. Self-learning is promoted in the organization providing sufficient learning resources.

Certification : It incorporates valid and reliable certification criteria and procedure for certification of competency.

Continuously Updated : The training plan is refined, modified, diversified and re-engineered based on the systematic training evaluation study and feedback of employees and stakeholders.

11. Training Management Team

A team manages the training programmes in the organization. This team of professionals and experts is responsible for management of the training. This team comprises members drawn from various key areas of the business, experts of training field and resource persons. The composition of training management team is shown in Fig. 7.5.

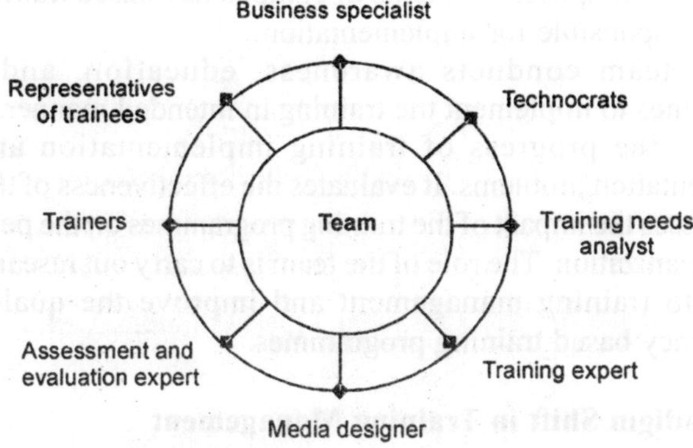

Fig. 7.5 : Training Management Team

The team is formed considering the needs of the training. If the organization is reengineering the management of training a core team is formed for this purpose and it is supported by various teams for carrying out major activities such as training needs analysis, training design, learning resources design, creating infrastructure, designing assessment and evaluation scheme, training policy formulation etc. The support teams disperse after completing their activities. The training design team of professionals and experts is drawn from various disciplines such as technologist, engineering educationalist, industry expert, psychologist/andragogist, expert trainers, evaluation expert, learning resources designers and so on.

The training management team has a vision to design competency-based training. The team designs and carries out the research study to design the training. If the organization is having well designed training management system in place there is no need to carry out the reengineering but it can take the help of experts for various purposes. If the competency based training is designed for the first time the study is carried out in detail to document related aspects of the organization and corporate world. If the training is designed second or third time there is no need to carry out the detailed research study. The snap study would serve the purpose along with inputs from training evaluation report, audit report and feedback from the management, trainees and other stakeholders.

The training management team designs the training systems, assures quality, adds value to training, and manages training programmes systematically and scientifically. The training design team propagates the spirit and intents of competency based training among trainers responsible for implementation.

The team conducts awareness, education, and training programmes to implement the training in intended manner. The team monitors the progress of training implementation and solves implementation problems. It evaluates the effectiveness of the training and assesses the impact of the training programmes on the performance of the organization. The role of the team is to carry out research studies related to training management and improve the quality of the competency based training programmes.

12. Paradigm Shift in Training Management

The developments in the field of training and competency development has compelled the training centres to shift from current practices to new practices. The paradigm shift required in training management is briefly stated in Fig. 7.6.

Fig. 7.6 : Paradigm Shift in Life Cycle of Training

Criteria	*Current practices*	*Practices of 21st century*
Training needs analysis		
Purpose	Solve problems	Solve problems and implement innovations
Approach	Reactive Casual	Proactive Scientific and systematic
Focus	Present Organization	Future Organization and environment
Time	One time activity	Continuous activity
Based on	Content, Gaps, Generalized approach	Core competency Gaps and new requirements Specific approach'
Training design		
Philosophy	Designed by experienced trainers	Designed by professionals and stakeholders including trainers
Approach	Blueprint approach Job and task analysis	Process approach Role analysis, organizational analysis, innovation plans and

Fig. 7.6 : (*Contd.*)

Criteria	*Current practices*	*Practices of 21st century*
	Present and near future considerations Principles of educational psychology Principles of training Supply driven, No benchmarking	major changes Vision consideration Principles of andragogy Principles of learning Demand driven Benchmarking with the best
Focus	Trainer, Content, Content and skills testing, Broad based	Trainees, Competency development Demonstration of competency Specific
Duration	Rigid Fixed	Flexible
Responsibility of learning	Trainer	Trainees
Training implementation		
Implementation plan	Generally not prepared Trainers rely on their experiences	Cluster of competency/competency plan is prepared
Learning resources	Ready made	Developed according to requirements of competency
Competency offerings	Rigid	Multiple and flexible options
Learning	Passive learning	Active learning
Role of trainer	Directive	Participative
Motivation	Trainer influences the behaviour of the trainees	Promote self motivation for learning
Power	Trainer enjoy administrative and expert power	Empower trainees for learning, Learning to learn concept is promoted
Emphasis	Topics completion	Learning about changing business, innovation, and development
Trainers think	Trainees need to be controlled	Trainees have potential to learn on their own, if properly guided
Recognition	Trainers take credit for the success	Trainees take credit for success
Rewards	Extrinsic	Extrinsic and intrinsic

Fig. 7.6 : (*Contd.*)

Criteria	*Current practices*	*Practices of 21st century*
Information	Controlled information	Fee flow of information
Problems	Trainers own the problem	Trainees own the problem.
Communication	Often one way	Multi channels of communication are used
Creativity and innovation	Less scope Analytical thinking	Foster creativity in learning, Promote thinking skills and
Perspective for development	Limited scope	Lifelong learning
Learning methods	Trainer centred methd Input based	Trainees centred methods Output based
Use of media	Traditional	Multi media
Way of learning	Formal	Formal and informal
Outcome of learning	Completing the training and appearing in test	Learning for life
Training evaluation		
Method	No scientific method is used based on formal and informal feedback Impact assessment is totally missing	Evaluation is based on well defined criteria such as: improvement in performance, improvement in result, increase in profit, expansion of business, satisfaction of customers, enhancement of corporate culture etc. Impact assessment
Life cycle of revision of training programmes	Very long	As short as significant changes in corporate world

13. Summary

- The corporate world is changing at a faster rate in all the dimensions of the business.
- The organization develops the professionals and employees

for changing needs of the business so that they can professionally perform the role in any situation, at any place and in any culture, under any conditions without much of anxiety, tension and stress.

- The organizations expect from its employees to satisfy and delight the customers. The professionals can perform professionally in the organization if the training programmes are designed, implemented and evaluated professionally.
- The training programmes are scientifically designed in order to prepare professionals for changing world.
- The role of the professionals in the organization is listed, prioritized and classified conducting a training needs identification research study.
- The competencies are derived from the role and competency map is prepared using vertical, horizontal and diagonal linkages.
- The affiliated competencies are clubbed together and learning process is designed for the cluster of competencies/ independent competencies.
- The current competency gaps are identified. The competencies to do business in future are also identified. The training programmes are designed to achieve these competencies.
- The learning process is designed in a way to ensure attainment of associative and peripheral competencies.
- Learning methods and resources are allocated to learning process and physical resources are organized to implement the learning process.
- The competencies of the trainees are tested and certified using well defined criteria and performance parameters.
- A team of experts drawn from various disciplines manage the training programmes.

14. Formats

Formate 7.1: *Examination of Competency-Based Training Programmes*

Training plans of competency-based programmes can be assessed on the criteria listed in the column two of the Format 7.1. The quality, effectiveness, efficiency and relevance of training plan can be assessed on 4-point scale. If the training gaps are very high assign 3, if it is high assign 2, if it is low assign 1 and if there is no gap assign 0. In the column number 4, list down the specific gaps. Think about strategies to minimize the gaps, reduce the deficiencies, remove the weaknesses and value addition in training design and mention them in column number 5.

Examination Sheet for Competency Based Training Programmes

Sl. No.	*Criteria*	*Extent of gaps*	*Nature of Gaps*	*Strategies to bring improvement*
1	*2*	*3*	*4*	*5*
1.	Rationale of the training			
2.	List of positions in the organization			
3.	Roles performed/to be performed by each position holder in the organization			
4.	Aim and scope of training programmes			
5.	List of departments/ sections where trained person can work			
6.	Classification of competencies			
7.	Competency maps			
8.	Credits or weightage for each competency			
9.	Proficiency level in each competency			
10.	Learning process			
11.	Learning methods			
12.	Learning resources			
13.	Learning experiences and opportunities			
14.	Flexibility in learning with respect to entry, time, duration, exit			
15.	Method for assessment of learning			
16.	Method of certification			
17.	Method of recognition of prior learning			
18.	Training implementation plan			
19.	The training design team			
20.	Method of training design			
21.	Mechanism to solve training implementation problems			

Sl. No.	Criteria	Extent of gaps	Nature of Gaps	Strategies to bring improvement
1	2	3	4	5
22.	Assumptions in design of the training			
23.	Role of trainers for implementation, assessment of learning and certification			
24.	Competence of trainers			
25.	Training of trainers			
26.	Procedure of training record management			
27.	Competency certifying agency			
28.	Support facilities for implementation			
29.	Role of corporate companies, industries, resource institutions, research institutions, and profesional body in training management			

15. Review Questions

1. Define training.
2. State the benefits of training at micro level.
3. State the benefits of training at macro level.
4. State the benefits of training at mega level.
5. State the benefits of training at meta level.
6. Describe the characteristics of training.
7. Explain the training management model.
8. Describe the functions of stakeholders in training management.
9. Explain the meaning of competency based training programmes.
10. List the importance of competency based training programmes.
11. Explain the purpose of competency based training programmes.
12. Compare the traditional training programmes with competency based training programmes.
13. Describe the characteristics of competency based training programmes.
14. State the composition of training management team.
15. Explain the paradigm shift required in training.

16. Activities for HR Managers

Examine the training plan of your organization on criteria stated in Format 7.1.

8

Competency Based Performance Review

LEARNING OBJECTIVES

After reading this chapter the readers will be able to :

- State the concept of performance appraisal.
- Use competency for performance review.
- Describe model of performance appraisal.
- State the decisions taken on the basis of competency based performance appraisal.

1. Introduction

The performance of the organization depends on the performance of the employees and other significant members involved in carrying out the business. The performance of key persons should be traced, monitored and measured to ascertain the quality of products and services of the organization. The performance appraisal system followed in many organizations is not based on scientific methods of planning, implementation and evaluation. Now competency based performance appraisal model based on scientific principles is available and in use. These models can be adopted and used in different organizations.

There is a need of a system that continuously monitors the progress of performance qualitatively and quantitatively. This is necessary for the growth and development of the employees and teams and at the same time for achieving the excellence. The growth and development of teams is possible in the appraisal situation where progress is monitored and underlying causes are identified for the poor performance or excellent performance. These causes are used to design the strategies to improve the performance of individuals and teams. Individuals and teams constantly improve the methods for improving the performance. Now-a-days use of information technology has become mandatory to enhance the performance of individuals and teams.

There is a need to derive the role of different position holders as well as teams keeping in view the roles prescribed by statutory body, stakeholders' expectations, organizational requirements and individual requirements. Role so derived should be appropriately allocated to the individuals and teams according to their competencies, capabilities, experience and willingness. Individuals and teams' performance should be measured on goals or objectives set by them against these roles.

2. Emerging Concepts of Performance Appraisal

Performance appraisal system has been used for a long time in various forms. Its definition and purpose changed time to time. The author proposes the following definitions :

- It is an instrument of assessing the performance of individuals and teams and to take decisions to enhance their effectiveness and efficiency within current environment with available resources.
- It is a system derived on the basis of strategic, perspective and tactical plan of the organization to develop the capacity and capability of employees to implement the organizational plans to achieve the vision, missions, goals and objectives.
- It is a tool to give rewards and create opportunities for the employees to develop themselves to their full potential.
- It is a system to define the scope of the work in terms of roles and responsibilities of the employees and develop them to perform professionally.
- It is a tool for deciding and organizing employee development programmes and creating attractive rewards for good performers.
- It is a proactive process of planning the performance and performing to achieve the challenging objectives.
- It is a process of learning from feedback of the self and stakeholders on the quality of performance and to improve performance.
- It is a process of creating and grabbing opportunities for professional development.

- It is a process of mutual, collaborative, cooperative and action learning in which all the employees participate with positive attitude to learn and enhance the work climate of the organization, to face the challenges and competitions.
- It is a prerequisite process performed by the organization that becomes base for taking significant decisions such as training, counseling, guidance, and coaching of individuals and teams.

3. Use of Comepetency for Performance Appraisal

The competencies are used in appraising the performance of individuals and teams. The competency profile of individuals and teams can be used to know their strengths and weaknesses with respect to their goals and roles.

Performance Planning

The individual employees know their competency profile related to their respective position or role. They know the strengths and weaknesses from their competency profile. They are also aware about the goals and priorities of the organization because they had participated in planning process and they know the plans for the year. Generally these plans are prepared on performance appraisal format because the formats work as a planning, implementation, monitoring and assessment sheet.

Considering their strengths and organizational priorities, they prepare individual plans for performance. For example, a professor is aware from her/his competency profile that she/he is possessing research competencies. She/he would like to set more research related goals in comparison to other role dimensions such as teaching learning, continuing education, extension, consultancy, and instructional material development. In research area she/he will be able to achieve the goals effectively and efficiently without any stress. She/he will be able to perform and achieve the goals under all limitations of the organization. She/he will not require external motivation for achieving the goals because of intrinsic motivation. It means competency profile is useful in planning the performance goals, setting priorities and preparing the performance plans.

Performance

The competency profile is also useful in implementing the plan because the performer is confident about her/his competencies. She/he will be able to mobilize the resources to implement the plan and achieve the goals. It is also useful in receiving self feedback on the progress and quality of performance because of internalized competency and proficiency. In such a situation close supervision and monitoring of the performance by superiors is not required. It saves the time spent by superiors on guiding, counseling, coaching, training, mentoring, solving problems and giving feedback.

Performance Evaluation

In performance evaluation the individuals get an opportunity to self evaluate their performance of the year against the planned goals. The performance is also evaluated by other stakeholders such as superiors, colleagues, subordinates, customers and other stakeholders. They also give recognition for excellent performance and provide constructive, positive, and development oriented feedback on areas of improvement. The individuals get satisfaction because they achieve goals according to plan. They are conscious about performance so they refine the competencies. This enriched experience of identifying the strengths, preparing plan, implementing plan, monitoring progress and evaluating achievement of goals is used in next cycle of performance management for improving the performance. The experience is positive so the competencies and proficiency get refined during the whole cycle of performance management.

The employees get immense level of internal satisfaction and they may get rewards for excellent performance. During this phase of performance management they may explore new potential on competency which can be used in next cycle of performance management. In next cycle they may set higher and challenging goals and easily achieve them. So using competency framework and profile provides a strong base for performance appraisal.

During performance appraisal process the formative and summative appraisal analysis may result in deficiency in competency of individuals or group of employees, and identification of new and higher level of competencies. On the basis of these results the competency profile of individuals and competency framework at organizational level may be refined.

Analysis of Performance Evaluation

The analysis of performance evaluation results at organizational level is useful for taking decisions such as training areas for different position holders, redeployment of individuals, promotion, career advancement, awarding new assignments, counseling, giving incentives, refining competency framework and profile, updating the competency profile, training management, budget allocation for HR interventions, etc.

4. Competency Based Planning at Organizational Level

The role related competencies are identified by position holders. Generally, these are mentioned in the competency manual of the organization. As mentioned earlier in chapter 1 that the individuals develop their competency profile against these competencies. In this profile the competencies are classified and prioritized. The structure of classification is also described in Chapter 1.

The method and criteria of classification depends on type of organization, level of professionalism, type of role and priorities of the organization. For school teachers the competencies are stated in three classifications such as curricular, co-curricular, extra-curricular. For college level teachers the classification is stated in nine areas such as academic, research, instructional resources development, continuing education, consultancy, extension, administration, management, and finance.

The competencies are listed for all the areas of classification for a particular role. But everyone performing the role is not expected to perform on all the dimensions and competencies equally and may not possess competency and proficiency at the same level. The individuals may possess different competencies and proficiency at different levels. Different role holders performing the same role may decide different priority among areas considering their strengths for preparing the plans. As a whole the summation of plans of all the individuals should meet the requirements of the plans of the organization that is why participative planning is carried out at organizational level to make minor adjustments on individual plans.

This approach of role and competency based planning is superior to simple participative planning at organization level. This approach of planning reduces cost, efforts and time required on training, guiding, coaching, counseling and mentoring because the strengths of individuals are used in planning and their weaknesses are covered up. This is a good method of assuring the professional performance with available resources in the organization.

5. Assessment of Competency in Performance Appraisal

There is a direct relationship between competency and performance. The level of competency and proficiency can be assessed through achievements. If an employee successfully achieves the planned goals it means the employee possess competencies and proficiency to perform a particular role. As stated earlier the performance is assessed on process and product.

The process assessment is useful to certify that the role has been performed effectively and efficiently. It means the performers used right method, tools, techniques, relationship behaviour, organizational norms etc. They have performed the role in right way. The product assessment is useful to certify that the performers have achieved the goals maintaining the quality of the product and services.

Process Assessment

It is generally carried out by self, superiors, peers and the internal customers. It is conducted during the performance using well designed observation sheet or check sheet according to requirement of the competency. The significant and direct parameters are identified and organized in the observation sheet. Generally, 3 to 7 point rating scale is used to rate the quality of performance. It is interesting to note here that subjectivity is converted into objectivity using observation sheet or check sheet.

The rating of self, peers, superiors, internal customers can be plotted on spider diagram to know the consistency among the raters, if the parameters of observation are same for all the raters. If parameters are different in that case it is difficult to compare the rating of different observers. It is suggested here that for the sake of comparison all the raters should not rate the process of performance. They should rate the process of performance related to their stake. For example, the following processes related competencies of the teacher can only be rated by self and students :

- Communicate effectively to explain the concepts, principles, processes, rules, etc.;
- Use information communication technology to make the learning joyful;
- Diagnose the learning problems of the students timely;
- Provide timely feedback on progress of learning;
- Create healthy learning environment in the classroom; and
- Use variety of teaching learning methods and media.

The other persons like head of department, principal, subordinates should not rate the performance of the teachers on these competencies based on secondary information. If all the students rate excellent on the above competencies, it means the quality of performance is excellent and *vice versa*. If average is worked out extreme cases (may be because of biasness) should be ignored in calculating the average. If the quality of process performance for a person is excellent or very good, she/he should be encouraged to achieve higher quality standards. She/he should be provided more opportunities for using these competencies.

If the process performance is poor in such a case the organizational, personal and environmental factors should be analyzed. This can be done comparing the performance with similar roles. If there is problem with these factors they should be removed designing and implementing appropriate strategies. If these factors are all right then the decisions should be taken to improve the performance of individuals. Various strategies such as counseling sessions, feedback sessions, training, coaching, mentoring, role shifting, socio-psycho support, etc. are used to improve the performance of poor performers.

There are chances of identifying potential for developing other competencies related to process of performance in employees. For example, a teacher is using research approach to improve the quality of teaching learning in the classroom. She/he is not aware about research methodology. She can be trained to develop this competency for further use. There are chances that during the process assessment potential for altogether different competency may be identified for a particular person. For example, a teacher possesses visionary ability which is identified during the process appraisal. This can be further developed through training and self learning and that teacher can be redeployed for school level planning.

The process assessment should also be used for creating learning opportunities for persons performing similar roles. They should be given an opportunity to share experiences related to quality of performance, generate innovative ideas to improve quality of performance and prevent problems related to quality of performance. These types of opportunities will help the role holders to refine their competencies related to process of performance.

Product Assessment

It is generally carried out by self, superiors, customers, peers and subordinates. Generally, it is based on facts and carried out against the planned goals. It is carried out on quantitative and qualitative parameters of the product. The appraisee reports the quantitative and qualitative planned goals and achievements against the same. If there is no gap between planned and achieved goals it can be concluded that the person has professionally performed. If the achievements are more than the planned, the planning process should be reviewed and accordingly decisions should be taken.

If achievements are less than planned, the environment, organizational and individual factors should be analyzed to design appropriate strategies for the future. If it is related to competency deficiency, training should be organized, if it is related to willingness guidance, counseling, mentoring should be organized, if it is related to organizational factors appropriate decisions should be taken, if it is related to environment, organizational strategy should be designed to deal with external forces.

6. Decisions Based on Process and Product Assessment

The appraisers and appraisee produce lot of information during process and product assessment of performance. This information is used for following purposes :

Refine the Competency Framework

On the basis of performance appraisal results the conclusions can be drawn on the competencies required and competencies used during the performance. If the performance gap is significant between competencies required and performed at organizational, department and section level one can conclude that there is a need to develop new competencies in the employees so that performance gap can be reduced or there is a need of refining the existing competencies.

Refine the Competency Profile

On the basis of performance appraisal results, if the performance of a particular group of roles is poor it should be analyzed and their competency profile should be updated or refined. Based on the upgraded competency profile the individuals should be allocated roles according to their strengths. If no option is available in role allocation the individuals are trained to develop specific competency and then they are assigned the role.

Identify the Gaps in Performance

The performance gap is identified on competency and proficiency and accordingly decisions are taken for training, guidance, coaching and mentoring. The performance of newly recruited person is closely monitored on competencies. They do not have habit of performing professionally because of new situation and lack of experience.

Identify the Training and Development Needs

The process assessment is useful in identifying the training and development needs of individuals and teams. The training is generally required to refine the competency and increase the proficiency. This is required when the person is redeployed or promoted or assigned additional role dimensions. The training needs are mentioned in terms of competency and proficiency gap and priority is also decided. It is generally identified in core competencies.

Know the Level of Competency and Proficiency

The level of competency and proficiency is required for taking significant decisions such as giving promotion, redeployment, giving additional responsibilities, role enrichment, role rotation, role redesign. If the level of competency and proficiency is known the person can be placed at right position. This will increase the productivity and satisfaction level of the person. It is useful for career advancement and development of the individuals.

Know the Potential to Develop New Competency

Every human being is different in personality. The individuals develop competencies through education, training, and experience. They pursue the career related to their competencies. They may do well on current roles. But the organization may be expanding the business or adopting the technology or diversifying from the current business. In such conditions there is a need to know the potential of individuals for developing new, different and advance competencies. The potential of individuals can be assessed for such competencies providing them an opportunity to work in real life or simulated situations.

Deploy and Redeploy the Employees

The organizations work in changing external and internal environment. They have to make adjustment with changing conditions. They cannot employ persons for each and every job. They have to deploy and redeploy the existing manpower to perform changing roles. The competency framework and profile is useful to deploy and redeploy the persons. The competency based deployment and redeployment decisions assure the professional performance. If people are deployed on the basis of experience, perception and opinion they need to be trained to develop the competency of new position. This may consume time, money and efforts. They may commit serious mistakes also.

Designing HR Interventions

The organization takes many decisions to enhance its effectiveness and efficiency. Many decisions may be related to human resources mobilization. Otherwise also other decisions affect the human resources mobilization. These decisions may be related to promotion, hiring, retaining, training, incentives, transfer and so on. The organization can take objective decisions on the basis of current assessment results.

Hire Consultants

There are a number of roles which are required to be performed for a particular period of time or tasks. The organization cannot employ a person or group of persons on permanent basis because after the task is over they may become redundant. For example, developing a software or designing a new building, designing a performance appraisal or audit system and so on. The updated competency framework and profile is useful to take decision about redeploying a person or hiring a person. The right person can be hired on the basis of competency profile.

Take Policy Decisions

The organization can take policy decisions on the basis of performance assessment. These may be related to promotion, training, counseling, mentoring, self-development, incentives, salary rise, and so on. These decisions may be related to performance appraisal itself.

7. Summary

- The performance of employees is directly proportional to the competencies possessed by them.
- The performance of the employees needs to be planned, monitored and reviewed at significant points to ensure the achievement of goals of the organization.
- The competency framework, competency profile and competency map is used for performance planning, implementation and evaluation.
- At organizational level competency based performance review is useful to allocate right role to right person and accordingly monitor the progress of the performance.
- The process review of performance is carried out to assess the quality of performance and improve the performance of individuals continuously updating the competency.
- There are some competencies which can only be assessed during performance.
- The product assessment is carried out to ascertain the overall performance in qualitative and quantitative terms.

- Process and product assessment is useful for taking significant decisions at organizational level.

8. Review Questions

1. State the concept of performance review.
2. State the concept of performance appraisal.
3. Differentiate between performance review and performance appraisal in the context of competency based performance review.
4. State the use of competency for performance appraisal.
5. Explain the support provided by competency profile for performance planning at organizational level.
6. How does competency profile facilitate the role performance at organizational level?
7. List the benefits of competency based planning at organizational level.
8. Differentiate process assessment and product assessment on points such as purpose, process, tools, decisions etc.
9. State five competencies which can be assessed using process assessment.
10. State five competencies which can be assessed using product assessment only.
11. List the decisions taken based on performance review at organizational level.

9. Activities for HR Managers

Activity 8.1: Design process assessment tools for one key role of your organization.

Activity 8.2: Design product assessment tools for one key role of your organization.

Activity 8.3: Design a competency based performance appraisal format for one key role of your organization.

9

Role of Human Resource Managers

LEARNING OBJECTIVES

After reading this chapter the readers will be able to :

- State the need of human resources (HR) manager in the context of managing competency based HR processes.
- Describe the Role of HR manager.
- State the behaviour of HR managers.
- State the competency profile of HR manager.
- List the training needs of HR manager.

1. Introduction

The behaviour of professionals and employees is influenced by human beings only. In all the organizations human beings are developed and deployed by HR department to produce super performance. The HR managers manage various HR functions and processes in the organization so that individual and collective intelligence and energy of people are mobilized to achieve the organizational goals, missions and vision at the same time the employees are satisfied and customers are delighted. The HR department designs and uses various strategies for developing the full potential of individuals and teams and utilizing it for the benefit of the organization.

The HR managers are trained in professionally managing the HR functions of the organization. They are expert in human resources planning, implementing plans and evaluating the impact of HR plans. To manage HR functions of the organization they perform wide spectrum of roles. On the basis of their roles and responsibilities, they are recruited, trained, deployed, retrained and redeployed. In this chapter role of HR manager is described with reference to competency framework.

2. Role of the HR Managers

The role of the HR managers in any organization depends on many internal and external factors. These factors are stated below :

The phase of life of the organization is a key factor in deciding the role of the HR manager. If the organization is at infancy stage, it is very difficult to define the role of the HR manager. At this phase the promoters of the business are not clear on HR functions. In many situations they take the services of the experts and external agency. If the first recruitment is effective then the organization develops otherwise trouble starts right from the beginning.

The type of the business of the organization is second factor to decide the role of the HR manager. If the organization is in dynamic and changing business the role of the HR manager becomes very important. If it is stable the role becomes routine.

If the organization is facing throat cutting competition and frequently implementing change and innovations to meet the competition and delight the current customers in such situations the role of the HR managers is dynamic and changing. The HR managers are required to work with close collaboration with other departments of the organization. The HR managers are required to update themselves with the changing expectations of internal and external customers and develop themselves to meet the expectations.

If the organization is at the stage of expansion of the same business and adding features in the products, in such situation the HR managers are required to recruit or hire or deploy the professionals. They get involved in orientation, training, and development activities. If organization *wide* technological change is being implemented in a short duration of time, the HR managers are required to develop part time trainers to cope up with the situation.

It is clear that the role of HR managers in different organization will be different. But the common functions may be the same as stated below :

- Manpower planning according to the needs of the plans.
- Recruitment according to competency framework.
- Orientation programmes at all levels.
- Developing competency framework for the organization and individual profile of employees.
- Contributing in organizational planning.
- Role design for supporting the organizational plans.
- Deploying right person for right role.

- Managing performance review and feedback.
- Training for development and refinement of competency.
- Guidance, counseling, mentoring, coaching and feedback.
- Performance assessment.
- Managing rewards and incentives.
- Identifying the potential of employees.
- Training and redeployment.
- Promotion of right persons at right time for right role.
- Succession planning.
- Retirement.
- Manage family welfare activities of employees.
- Human resources information system.
- Role enrichment programmes.
- Organizational development programmes.
- Managing change and innovations.
- Building corporate culture.

3. Behaviour of HR Managers

The HR managers must possess behaviour aligned to the roles stated above. The inherent behaviour of the HR managers should be such as to develop themselves to become professional HR manager.

The HR managers are required to control their personal behaviour, opinion, suggestions, feelings and perceptions about the employees. They need to be self-disciplined so far their behaviour is concerned. They need to demonstrate behaviour, which is helpful to trainees for their empowerment. The professional HR managers demonstrate behaviour characteristics stated in Fig. 9.1.

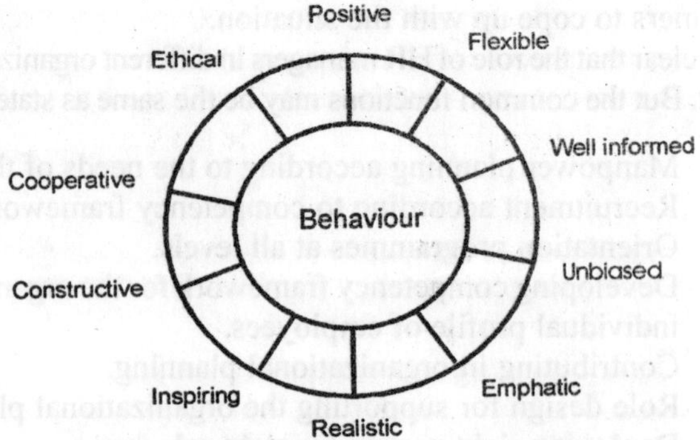

Fig. 9.1 : Characteristics of HR Managers

4. Competency Profile of HR Manager

The HR managers undertake the preparation of competency framework and competency profile for employees of the organization. They should be competent, proficient, effective and efficient in managing HR processes. They should possess set of competencies stated in competency profile of HR managers

Legend : E – Essential, D – Desirable, O – Optional, R – Routine, NR– Non-routine, I – Innovative, A – Associated

Sl. No.	*Competency Profile of HR managers*	*Type*
A.	**Identify the training needs**	**E, NR**
1.	Plan the training needs identification study	
2.	Design objectives of the study	
3.	Design methodology of the study	
4.	Design instruments of study	
5.	Select population and sample	
6.	Gather information	
7.	Analyze information	
8.	Draw conclusions and finalize training needs	
9.	Get approval from competent authority for training design	
B.	**Design training programme**	**E, R**
10.	Finalize the objectives of training	
11.	Design training/learning strategy	
12.	Select learning resources	
13.	Identify other resources to support implementation of training plan	
14.	Design assessment scheme	
C.	**Prepare for implementing training strategy**	**E, R**
15.	Prepare detailed competency development/ refinement plan	
16.	Design learning resources print such as text book, reference book, manual, reports, handouts, case studies, ready made games, anecdote, charts, etc.	
17.	Design learning resources non-print such as model, power point presentations, video lectures, video programmes, computer aided instructions and simulations, multimedia packages, e-books etc.	
18.	Decide techniques such as administering test, interview, role play, process observation, assignments, product assessment, etc.	
19.	Manage learning resources	
20.	Design assessment tools such as test, observation, schedule, check list, rating scale, interview schedule, exercise, etc.	

Sl. No.	*Competency Profile of HR managers*	*Type*
21.	Prepare session plan	
22.	Organize physical resources for conducting training programme	
D.	**Impart training**	E, R
23.	Deliver lectures to achieve learning objectives	
24.	Demonstrate process of operation	
25.	Conduct group discussions	
26.	Organize panel discussions	
27.	Organize focus group discussions	
28.	Organize seminar, conference and symposium for training	
29.	Facilitate action learning	
30.	Organize role play	
31.	Organize learning games	
32.	Organize competitions	
33.	Develop case studies	
34.	Use case studies	
35.	Organize simulations	
36.	Organize in-basket	
37.	Conduct on the job training	
38.	Conduct creativity sessions	
39.	Organize excursions	
40.	Conduct problem based learning sessions	
41.	Organize practical training	
42.	Design practice exercise	
43.	Design projects	
44.	Facilitate projects	
45.	Organize question-answer sessions	
46.	Guide self learning	
47.	Coach to develop specific competencies	
48.	Mentor selected employees	
49.	Conduct counseling sessions	
50.	Diagnose learning problems	
51.	Conduct tutorials	
52.	Maintain records of progress of learning	
E.	**Conduct assessment of learning**	E, R
53.	Conduct formative assessment	
54.	Conduct feedback sessions	
55.	Conduct assessment	
56.	Conduct assessment for certification of competency	
F.	**Prepare reports**	E, R
57.	Prepare completion report of training	
58.	Conduct research studies on various phases of training programme	
59.	Conduct action research	
60.	Conduct training impact study	

Sl. No.	Competency Profile of HR managers	Type
G.	**Design change and innovation**	D, NR
61.	Design change and innovation for improving the quality of training	
62.	Suggest non-training interventions for improving the performance of the organization	
63.	Use information communication technology in training	E, R
64.	Contribute in various organizational innovations for improving the business	E, NR, I
65.	Contribute in designing HR interventions	NR, I
66.	Conduct audit of training programmes	D, NR
67.	Organize seminar, conference and symposium for group of organization, professional body and other organizations for various purposes	NR, I
68.	Publish magazine of the organization	R, I
69.	Encourage organizational members for pursuing training and development activities	R, D
H.	**Self-development**	E, R
70.	Prepare self-development plan	
71.	Contribute in performance appraisal of self and other trainers	
I.	**Undertake consultancy**	O, NR
72.	Design training management proposals for other organisations	
73.	Conduct training programmes	
74.	Certify competencies	
75.	Conduct impact assessment	
J.	**Collaborate for managing training**	E, R
76.	Identify the stakeholders	
77.	Develop relationship with them	
78.	Involve them in managing training	
K.	**Develop competency framework**	E, NR
79.	Design a research study	
80.	Conduct research study	
81.	Report competency framework	
82.	Report competency profile for different roles	
83.	Prepare competency map	
84.	Update competency framework and competency profiles	E, R
L.	**Manage HR processes**	
85.	Design manpower deployment plans	
86.	Recruit professionals	
87.	Design succession plans	
88.	Design career advancement plans	
89.	Manage training and development	
90.	Organize performance review	
91.	Enrich various roles	

Sl. No.	*Competency Profile of HR managers*	*Type*
92.	Deploy and redeploy professionals	O
93.	Prepare HR policies	E, NR
94.	Update HR policies	
95.	Manage retirements	E, R
96.	Manage complaints of employees	E, R
97.	Hire consultants	D, NR
98.	Manage retrenchment	D, NR
99.	Organize career advancement opportunities	E, R
100.	Manage compensations	D, NR
101.	Recommend incentives	E, R
102.	Manage welfare of employees	E, R
M.	**Promote healthy culture and climate**	
103.	Socialize the permanent as well as temporary professionals	D, R
104.	Design organisational development interventions	
105.	Promote culture aligned to vision of the organization	
106.	Manage conflicts and litigations	
107.	Manage behavioural problems	E, R

5. Summary

- The behaviour of the employees can be influenced to achieve a specific purpose.
- In organizations HR managers recruit and develop employees for achieving organizational goals.
- The HR managers are trained to manage HR processes professionally.
- The role of HR managers depends on various internal and external factors. They have to perform on variety of role dimensions considering the requirement of the situation.
- The HR managers need to be positive, flexible, well informed, unbiased, emphatic, realistic, inspiring, constructive, cooperative and ethical.
- The profile of HR managers needs to be balanced on various functions of HR and roles to be performed.

6. Review Questions

1. State the role of HR managers.
2. List the characteristics of HR managers.
3. Compare the role of HR managers with production manager.

4. State the training needs of the HR managers.

7. Activities for HR Managers

Activity 9.1: Prepare a competency profile of all HR managers of your organization.

Activity 9.2: Prepare a competency profile of part time HR managers.

Frequently Asked Questions

Question 1 : If the organization is working traditionally and there are number of problems related to technology, finance, and processes, should the organization decide to develop and use competency framework ?

Response : Development of competency framework and its use is no solution for solving all types of problems of the organization. In such situation, it will not bring much impact on overall performance of the organization. In the opinion of the author the organization should design and introduce related changes such as technological, financial, processes etc. and side by side it can introduce competency framework based HR interventions. The framework will be dynamic till other changes are established.

Question 2 : Which approach of competency framework development is better whole to part or part to whole?

Response: The whole to part method is considered to be a better method to see the immediate and long term impact of competency framework. Again it depends on the size of the organization, purpose, time and money available for the project and other similar factors. The author recommends for whole to part with broad and generic focus in contrast to narrow and limited focus.

Question 3 : We do not have expertise in our organization for developing competency framework, should we assign this project to consultant ?

Response : There is no other person who knows your business than your own employees. So the competency framework development project should be undertaken participatively by a team drawn from your organization. It will help you to smoothly implement the framework for various purposes. You are always free to take services of consultants for guiding and supporting the team.

Question 4 : How elaborative the competency framework should be for any organization ?

Response : You can see from the examples of competency framework that it should be sufficient and necessary to communicate the requirements of abilities of human resources and design HR interventions to conduct the business effectively and efficiently. The larger number of competencies will prevent the HR department to see the whole HR requirements. It should contain minimum number of competencies covering every aspect so HR strategies can be designed effectively and efficiently. The detailing of the competencies can be done for identifying the training needs and designing training programmes. The detailing of competency is done either in sub-competencies or instructional objectives.

Question 5 : The top management of the organization is unaware about competency based human resources management. It is always interested in production and quality of products. It takes all the human resources development initiatives casually. How to cope up with such situations?

Response : The interest of top management is genuine. It is the responsibility of HR managers to prepare the compressive proposal for developing and using competency framework. This proposal should be presented to the top management at right time when the condition is highly favourable or unfavourable. They should be informed about the practices of sister organizations and competitors about human resources management.

Question 6 : The organizational structure is hierarchical and the authority is decentralized. Can we implement competency framework in such organization.

Response : The hierarchical structure and centralized authority delay the action and acts as barrier to change and development of the organization. The organizational structure should be continuously evolved to respond to changing needs of the customers incorporating technology and techniques in its functioning. It is suggested that the adequate autonomy should be granted to people and teams to achieve organizational goals. The organization should first redesign the roles, responsibilities, duties, and accountability and then develop and use competency framework.

Question 7 : The organization has employed professionals 15 years back. Now the complete business and way of doing the business has changed. They cannot be trained any more because of many inherent problems. How competency framework can help ?

Response : This is the major problem in companies doing business in new and emerging discipline. There are limits of training and development. The other options such as voluntary retirement, place them in low key areas, half pay leave etc. should be exercised. The young and competent professionals should be employed or hired for changed business.

Question 8 : Will the competency framework bring rigidity in the HR practices?

Response : No, certainly not. It will provide wider scope for scientifically designing and implementing the HR processes considering the limitations of the organization.

Question 9 : Can competency based HR interventions reduce turnover of employees ?

Response : Yes, it considers the strengths of employees in relation to business of the organization so the right persons can be redeployed if they are not satisfied with their current role. It will also provide base for negotiation on strengths and weaknesses of the employees in order to influence them.

Question 10 : Can competency framework development exercise become a base for bringing major HR changes ?

Response: Competency framework development is useful where the systems are in place. It works best when it is developed on well designed business and organization. The other way round will not bring much impact on the business.

Question 11 : The organization has recently revised the competency framework and now it wants to implement major change in the functioning of the organization. Should it redevelop the competency framework ?

Response : No, there is no need to redevelop competency framework because the major changes are related to the business itself. It can update the competency framework and competency profile of the individuals. It has to undertake training and development activities simultaneously in integrated manner to cope up with the change and sustain the interest of the employees.

Question 12 : I have attended one training programme on competency framework development and its use for human resources development. In that training programme more emphasis was given on job analysis approach. I think that is a very old approach for identifying the training needs.

Response : You are very correct. The job analysis approach is an old technique and it is used for specialized job only. Now the whole world is practicing the concepts of role, empowerment, accountability, multi skills development and role efficacy. As described in this book the role is the prerequisite for competency framework development. There is no need to go in much detail while developing or analyzing the roles. The competencies can be derived from the role itself. For more information please refer the process of competency framework development given in this book. The job analysis is used for designing the training programmes for specialized competency where the job can make or break the life of people.

Question 13 : How competency framework improves the work culture of the organization ?

Response : The employees know about their roles and level of competencies possessed by them. They know the strengths and weaknesses of each other. They seek mutual help for performing the role wherever they are weak. The competency framework provides the base for mutual training, development, guidance, counseling, coaching and appreciation. It improves the effectiveness of communication among employees. It guides the HR managers to design and implement strategies which improve the productivity as well as work culture of the organization.

Question 14 : Can there be different levels of competency and proficiency?

Response : Yes, the level of competency may be different at different levels and different point of time. For example, the leadership at operational level team is different than leadership at organizational level. Similarly at operational level routine decisions are taken but at organizational level non-routine policy decisions are taken. Routine decisions are simply reviewed at organizational level. The proficiency at competency level is also defined to express proficiency level of the employees. The proficiency may be different for different levels and situations.

Question 15 : Can we repeat the competency in competency framework ?

Response : No, in competency framework the competencies are identified and stated once in generic terms. At competency profile level they can be defined considering the requirement of the role and position. Similarly, the proficiency is also indicated at role level wherever it is necessary to qualify the competency.

Question 16 : Can competency profile be used for training design?

Response : Competency profile of individuals is the base for identifying, designing and implementing the training. Generally the orientation programmes are designed and implemented based on the competency profile. The competency profile is used by individuals for self-development. It is used for guidance, coaching and mentoring by superiors. It is used for giving and receiving feedback for mutual improvement.

Question 17 : How do we assess the competency of professionals ? Is it similar to assessing the competencies in educational institutions ?

Response : The assessment of competency in organization is different than assessment of competency in educational institutions. In educational institutions the focus is learning and acquiring the competency so the focus of assessment is different. In organizations the employees keep record of evidences of demonstration of competencies. These records are shown at the time of assessment of competency. The competency is assessed on significant and direct indicators using principle of necessary and sufficient evidences.

Question 18 : What are the sources of competency framework development ?

Response : The organization's vision document, strategic plans, reports, problems faced, policies, trends in business, experts, competitors, challenges etc. are the sources of information for competency framework development.

Question 19 : Which techniques are used for identifying training needs ?

Response : The self analysis of performance, peer assessment and observation by superiors against competency profile are the frequently used techniques.

Question 20 : What is the unique feature of the competency framework?

Response : The unique feature of competency framework is that it is aligned with core business of the organization and indicates that if sum total of competencies of all professionals is equal in quantity and quality it would enable the professionals to perform professionally in present and near future in order to achieve the challenging goals of the organization.

Question 21 : How many competencies should be there in a competency framework for an organization ?

Response : We have experienced that in a generic competency framework there could be 10 to 50 core competencies, 5 to 20 associative competencies, 5 to 25 peripheral competencies and other competencies according to needs of the organization. Although the number of competencies depend on size, spectrum, geographic spread and type of the business.

Examples of Competency Framework and Competency Profile

LEGEND FOR CLASSIFYING THE COMPETENCIES

E — Essential, D — Desirable, O — Optional, R — Routine, NR — Non-routine, I — Innovative, A — Associated, P — Present, PPL — Peripheral, ENG — Engineering, M — Managerial, C — Change management, SD — Staff development. T — Threshold, DIF — Differentiating, ELE — Elemental, G-Generic, MT — Meta, CEN — Central, S — Surface

1. Competency Framework for Corporate Office

Sl .No.	*Competency framework*	*Type*
1.	Frame policies to enhance profit, net worth and wealth of the organization to make it financially independent	E
2.	Monitor the progress of the regional, district and other units and provide proper guidance	R, E
3.	Issue clear orders and instructions	E, R
4.	Solve problems communicated by regional, district and other units timely	E, R
5.	Ensure participation in target setting	D
6.	Ensure financial and administrative discipline at all levels.	D
7.	Ensure effective implementation of existing projects, programmes and activities	E, R
8.	Select new projects, programmes and activities with high return	C
9.	Make the provision of sufficient fund, facilities and support to conduct business and render required services	E, R
10.	Devise human resources development policy and ensure its implementation	E, NR
11.	Provide effective leadership	E
12.	Make timely decisions	D
13.	Involve related units in significant decision making processes	D
14.	Boost the morale of the employees of the organization	D
15.	Update all policies involving employees	D

Sl No.	*Competency framework*	*Type*
16.	Decentralize administrative and financial powers	D
17.	Equip Regional and Branch office with sufficient staff and resources	E
18.	Collaborate with stakeholders for different business ventures	E
19.	Bring transparency in the working of the organization	D
20.	Promote team work in the organization	D
21.	Enhance work culture and working environment	PPL
22.	Make available quality services/product timely as per needs and expectations of the customers at reasonable price	E
23.	Attempt in various business dimensions to bring developments in the organization	CEN
24.	Provide required information about the organization to stakeholders and related others	E
25.	Emphasize on helping relationship with stakeholders	D
26.	Establish management information system and ensure its effective use by all concerned	D
27.	Ensure effective cash management and inventory control at all levels	E
28.	Ensure recovery of all outstanding and reduce instances of bad debt cases	E
29.	Ensure financial viability of all units	E
30.	Eliminate unproductive expenditure	E
31.	Promote self-appraisal of all activities	D
32.	Ensure employee satisfaction in the organization	D
33.	Experiment with new/innovative ventures	I
34.	Launch own quality products in the market as per market demand	D
35.	Ensure stable market of products and services	E
36.	Decide inducements/incentives timely to promote market share	E
37.	Take up market research regularly	R
38.	Obtain services of non-government organizations in the field where they are expert	O
39.	Establish a network of stakeholders for mutual benefit	D

2. Competency Framework of Regional Office

Sl. No.	*Competency framework of regional office*	*Type*
1.	Ensure achievement of agreed targets	E
2.	Ensure the timely implementation of various corporate projects and sachemes	E
3.	Ensure implementation of organisational policy in its true spirit	R
4.	Exercise administrative control in all units of the division	E, R

Sl. No.	*Competency framework of regional office*	*Type*
5.	Exercise financial control in all units	E, R
6.	Timely report to headquarters	R
7.	Establish network with other related government officers at divisional and district level	D
8.	Coordinate and collaborate with allied agencies	D
9.	Procure required material in time	E, R
10.	Accord administrative and financial approvals to subordinate office in time	E
11.	Periodically monitor the performances of branches	D
12.	Provide guidance to district managers as and when required	O
13.	Arrange extra support to district managers when needed	D
14.	Provide support of divisional officers in implementation of the schemes of field units	D
15.	Timely deal with complaints received from stakeholders and users effectively	E
16.	Solve problems of suppliers/manufactures and other in the context of the regional office	E, R
17.	Establish collaborative network with CCBs and cooperative societies	D
18.	Liaison with officers of cooperative banks at divisional level	D
19.	Ensure fulfilment of the expectations of financial institutions	D
20.	Devise regional marketing strategies and ensure its implementation	E
21.	Ensure timely after sale services	D
22.	Ensure timely release of payments to suppliers	D
23.	Ensure implementation of various policies and government schemes	D
24.	Resolve grievances of employees in time.	E, R
25.	Disseminate information about Agro to all related persons/agencies to enhance its image.	D, R
26.	Disseminate information about product and services of Agro	D, R
27.	Expand present marketing network	E
28.	Acquire and introduce new products in the market	E
29.	Educate customers through various means and modes	D
30.	Give suggestions to improve the product quality and services	D
31.	Involve opinion leaders in major thrusts	D
32.	Endeavour to build the image of the organisation	D
33.	Endeavour to develop image of an ideal regional unit	D
34.	Establish effective management information system and ensure its appropriate use	R
35.	Promote performance appraisal and staff development policy.	E, R

3. Competency Framework of Branch Office

Sl. No.	*Competency framework of Branch office*	*Type*
1.	Disseminate information to all related persons and agencies regarding the product and services	E, R
2.	Publicize the activities of Agro through various modes and methods	E
3.	Provide good quality of products and services to consumers/beneficiaries	E
4.	Provide after sales services as required or on demand	E
5.	Train consumers/beneficiaries regarding use of implements/equipments and their proper care	D, R
6.	Extend resource support for government schemes	D
7.	Utilize the subsidy fully	D
8.	Implement schemes effectively and efficiently	D
9.	Ensure timely supply of material to consumers	E
10.	Establish proper procedure of payment/transportation	E
11.	Give sufficient notice for supply of material	D
12.	Ensure proper protection and timely sale of material received	D
13.	Send required reports to regional office and Head Office in time	D
14.	Keep in regular contact with finance agencies.	D
15.	Promote congenial atmosphere among the competitors	D
16.	Involve opinion leaders in decision making	D
17.	Accomplish set targets	E
18.	Timely request for materials to regional office.	E
19.	Promote image of the Agro in their respective districts.	E
20.	Adhere to rules and regulations of the organisations.	E
21.	Meet the demand of different government departments.	D
22.	Collaborate with district agencies for promoting business	E
23.	Solve problems of suppliers related to Branch office in time	E
24.	Keep continuous live contact with farmers	D
25.	Seek guidance from regional office and headquarters in complex matters	D
26.	Promote area specific market research and its use for appropriate service/product mix	D
27.	Develop staff to enter in new business	E
28.	Reinforce management information system and use it appropriately	E
29.	Provide feedback on technology and techniques to regional office, head office and manufactures	D
30.	Promote team work at branch level	D

4. Competencies of an Entrepreneur

Sl. No.	Competency profile of an entrepreneur	Type
1.	Technical competencies related to enterprise	
2.	Establish intimate relationship with customers and significant stakeholders	
3.	Use creativity at different phases of enterprise with various purposes	
4.	Predict the need of the product and services	
5.	Manage change in the enterprise	
6.	Manage the stress of the self and employees	
7.	Win over the competition	
8.	Guide, coach, and mentor the employees for production and quality of products	
9.	Manage the resources of the enterprise	
10.	Lead the enterprise for excellence	
11.	Influence the customers for purchasing the products and services	
12.	Face the crisis	
13.	Build teams to achieve specific goals	
14.	Analyse the environment	
15.	Make effective decisions	
16.	Prepare strategic, perspective, and annual plans	
17.	Take risk	
18.	Manage time	
19.	Design marketing strategy	
20.	Learn new competencies	
21.	Analyse economic environment	
22.	Ensure customer satisfaction	
23.	Handle complaints	
24.	Remove grievances of employees	
25.	Manage stakeholders	

5. Competencies for Induction Training Programme Phase I

List of competencies for training the newly appointed teachers of engineering colleges in induction programme

Sl. No.	Competencies for induction training programme phase I	Type
1.	Use system's model in planning and managing the learning activities	
2.	Formulate learning objectives	
3.	Prepare lesson plan	
4.	Select alternative strategies to achieve learning objectives	
5.	Select alternative media for implementing the learning strategies	

Sl. No.	Competencies for induction training programme Phase I	Type
6.	Design and prepare instructional resources	
7.	Design variety of learning experiences	
8.	Conduct session according to plan	
9.	Communicate effectively to achieve learning objectives	
10.	Design different types of questions to diagnose learning problems and produce learning	
11.	Present new information through lecture	
12.	Demonstrate a process or functions of machine	
13.	Use reinforcement techniques to encourage students to learn further	
14.	Conduct group discussion	
15.	Use role playing and simulation	
16.	Direct students in applying problem solving techniques	
17.	Use project method	
18.	Guide laboratory experiences	
19.	Organize field trips	
20.	Facilitate creativity sessions	
21.	Guide self-learning	
22.	Lead team teaching	
23.	Conduct a seminar	
24.	Design library assignments	
25.	Design assessment tools and techniques	
26.	Assess the learning progress and learning outcome	
27.	Perform in institutional teams	
28.	Develop healthy environment for joyful learning	

6. Competencies for Induction Training Programmes Phase II

Sl. No.	Competencies for induction training programmes Phase II	Type
1.	Identify the potential of students	
2.	Participate in curriculum design process	
3.	Prepare subject plan	
4.	Design learning modules for self-learning	
5.	Design assessment scheme	
6.	Assess the effectiveness of teaching learning process	
7.	Assess learning progress of students	
8.	Guide students to solve academic and personal problems	
9.	Manage inventory to conduct practical and workshop practices	
10.	Use Information communication technology in teaching learning process	
11.	Increase utilization factor of human as well as physical resources	
12.	Develop professional relationship with other teachers and officers	
13.	Observe professional ethics	

Sl. No.	Competencies for induction training programmes Phase II	*Type*
14.	Develop management information system	
15.	Use advance methods of teaching learning	

7. Competencies for Relationship Building

Sl. No.	*Competencies for relationship building*	*Type*
1.	Explore opportunities for relationship building	
2.	Design strategies to develop relationship at organizational level	
3.	Develop contacts with individuals, teams and organization	
4.	Develop business relation with individuals, teams and organization	
5.	Enter in an agreement for mutual work and benefit	
6.	Seek cooperation and support to achieve mutually agreed goals	
7.	Work in joint teams	

8. Competencies for Managers

Sl. No.	*Competencies for managers*	*Type*
A.	Planning	
1.	Prepare plans for growth and development of the organization	
2.	Prepare routine plans for production	
3.	Prepare project plans	
4.	Prepare human resources development plans	
5.	Prepare change and innovation plans	
6.	Prepare monitoring and evaluation plans	
7.	Prepare resources deployment plans	
8.	Prepare maintenance plans	
9.	Prepare contingency plans	
10.	Prepare risk management plans	
11.	Prepare stakeholders management plans	
12.	Prepare performance appraisal plans	
13.	Prepare marketing plans	
14.	Prepare research plans	
B.	Organization	
15.	Organize all types of resources according to plans	
16.	Coordinate the activities of employees to produce quality products and services	
17.	Cooperate to other functionaries of the organization for achieving organizational goals	
C.	Supervision	
18.	Assess the progress of performance of subordinates quantitatively and qualitatively	

Sl. No.	*Competencies for managers*	*Type*
19.	Provide support to carry out the tasks according to plans	
20.	Help them solve day-to-day problems	
21.	Assure quality of products	
D.	**Leadership**	
22.	Lead the followers and teams to achieve the individual as well as organizational goals	
23.	Provide vision for the future business	
24.	Take initiatives to respond to changing needs of the customers	
E.	**Innovations**	
25.	Design innovations for improving and innovating the performance of the organization as a whole	
26.	Promote creativity in the functioning of the organization	
27.	Reward creative and innovative ideas of the employees	
28.	Encourage entrepreneurship at all levels of functioning	
F.	**Human resources development**	
29.	Develop the human resources according to the needs of the business	
30.	Create opportunities for self development	
31.	Guide, counsel, mentor and coach the subordinates for achieving various goals	
G.	**Team work**	
32.	Work in teams to achieve team goals	
33.	Observe team norms	
34.	Promote healthy, conducive and synergetic culture in the functioning of the team	
35.	Provide constructive, positive and development oriented feedback	
36.	Encourage the employees for achieving higher goals	
H.	**Empowerment**	
37.	Empower employees in various areas of functioning of the organization	
38.	Grant autonomy and flexibility in order to effectively achieve goals	
I.	**Decision making**	
39.	Take effective decisions to achieve goals	
40.	Design strategies to achieve the set goals	
J.	**Conflict management**	
41.	Manage all types of conflicts within and outside the organization	
42.	Negotiate with internal and external stakeholders	
K.	**Resources utilization**	
43.	Use all types of resources effectively and efficiently	

Sl. No.	*Competencies for managers*	*Type*
44.	**Update resources in order to effectively perform**	
45.	**Condemn obsolete resources**	
L.	**Communication**	
46.	**Communicate orally for achieving the organizational goals**	
47.	**Communicate in writing**	
48.	**Prepare reports**	
49.	**Manage information**	
50.	**Prepare all types of prescribed documents**	
51.	**Make presentations for various purposes**	
M.	**Role related competencies**	
52.	**Observe time deadlines**	
53.	**Take risk**	
54.	**Motivate others to achieve the goals**	
55.	**Assure quality of product and services**	
56.	**Show empathy for genuine problems of others**	
57.	**Feel personally responsible for achieving the goals**	
58.	**Maintain confidentiality of information wherever required by the law**	
59.	**Update self competencies according to needs of the role**	
60.	**Demonstrate emotional intelligence**	
61.	**Reduce waste of time, money and resources**	
62.	**Save energy and water**	
63.	**Conserve environment**	
64.	**Observe safety rules**	
65.	**Maintain self-identity**	
66.	**Take initiative in change management**	
67.	**Prevent problems**	
68.	**Maintain hygienic conditions**	
69.	**Demonstrate good human relationship**	
70.	**Aspire for achieving higher level goals**	
71.	**Demonstrate high level of confidence during performance**	
72.	**Maintain diary of experiences**	
73.	**Use free time effectively**	
74.	**Contribute in social and cultural activities**	
75.	**Update information continuously through reading, internet and other modes**	
76.	**Demonstrate cheerful behaviour to fellow members**	
77.	**Think positively even in worse situations**	

9. Competencies for Erection and Commissioning Division

Sl. No.	Competencies for erection and commissioning division	*Type*
1.	Intimate the concerned agency to dispatch the needed documents to documentation cell well in time	

Sl. No.	Competencies for erection and commissioning division	*Type*
2.	Supply the documents well in time to documentation centre	
3.	Take back the unrevised documents and supply the revised documents to documentation centre	
4.	Give the requirements of materials as per erection schedule to material management section	
5.	Assist material management section in inspection of incoming materials	
6.	Help in preparation of material discrepancy report	
7.	Report the damages of material to insurance company for refund	
8.	Supply documents related to erection and communication to the contractors in time	
9.	Manage inventory to supply the components for erection in time	
10.	Procure tools for erection	
11.	Prepare plans for erection process	
12.	Communicate to contractor about revision and modifications in documents and design well in time	
13.	Inspect the erection work carried out by contractor on completion	
14.	Make arrangements for monthly payment to workers/labour at site	
15.	Inform quality control department for stage-wise inspection	
16.	Adhere to the specifications during erection process	
17.	Help the quality control department in making protocol with customs	
18.	Provide the site action report wherever required	
19.	Ensure safety measures at site	
20.	Coordinate with safety personnel in preparation of accidental reports	
21.	Create awareness of safety at site using various modes.	
22.	Provide fire protection equipments whenever necessary	
23.	Arrange training programmes related to safety measures for employee	
24.	Maintain the quality standards as needed by customer	
25.	Work in accordance with the project schedule	
26.	Submit in advance the requirements for equipment and materials to facility engineer	
27.	Submit bills of customer and contractor well in advance to accounts departments	
28.	Coordinate with labour officer	
29.	Strictly enforce statutory obligation	
30.	Reward the individuals for their outstanding work	
31.	Create awareness regarding schedules, quality and productivity	
32.	Promote team work	

10. Competencies for erection division

Sl. No.	*Competencies for erection division*	*Type*
1.	Provide quality service as specified by customer	
2.	Communicate the budget, targets as well as material requirements to planning section in time.	
3.	Report the progress of work time to time to planning departments	
4.	Satisfy the quality control requirements with respect to the work done during erection	
5.	Maintain and update documentary evidence and protocols during erection work	
6.	Follow labour enforcement rules strictly	
7.	Maintain proper records of the labour engaged in erection work	
8.	Provide hospitality to labour officer	
9.	Make labour payments as per Labour Act.	
10.	Obtain prior approval for erection from boiler inspection	
11.	Erect pressure vessels as per rules	
12.	Take sub-contractor into confidence while doing the job	
13.	Make timely payments to sub-contractors	
14.	Make timely billing and collection so that it reaches regional headquarters in time	
15.	Work in the interest of organisation to achieve its set target	
16.	Take all financial approval from the competent authority	
17.	Report to headquarters regarding the progress of erection work	
18.	Follow safety rules	
19.	Make sure that workers wear the safety appliances	
20.	Provide the security for the equipments at erection site	
21.	Provide sufficient illumination at the site	
22.	Arrange transport facility as and when required	
23.	Use appropriate and tested tools and plants	
24.	Ensure proper maintenance of cranes	
25.	Use the equipment under the conditions specified in the manual	
26.	Fulfil the budget	
27.	Not over spend money for personal comfort	
28.	Purchase as per the procedure	
29.	Estimate materials needs as well as withdrawal from the stores	
30.	Inspect material as well as damages and report to material management section for claiming insurance	
31.	Check the quality of material	
32.	Claim insurance	

Sl. No.	*Competencies for erection division*	*Type*
33.	Satisfy customer expectations	
34.	Complete erection work in time	
35.	Prepare time schedule for dispatch of material	
36.	Coordinate activities of different team members	
37.	Chase up material from manufacturing unit	
38.	Effectively coordinate with customer on commercial matters	
39.	Extend cooperation to planning and material management	
40.	Take right decisions at right time	
41.	Resolve the problems of the section members at site only	
42.	Promote effective communication	
43.	Promote team spirit	
44.	Arrange for timely training	

11. Competencies for Project and IDS

Sl. No.	*Competencies for P and IDS*	*Type*
1.	Stick to the customer specification as per the contract	
2.	Submit the design document to the customer well in time	
3.	Obtain prior permission from the customer for any deviations in design	
4.	Get the vendors approved by the customers	
5.	Select vendor from customer approved list	
6.	Incorporate the suggestions/comments of the customers	
7.	Ensure performance of equipment as guaranteed by vendor	
8.	Furnish the plant parameters as early as possible to control and instrumentation department	
9.	Furnish data sheet and HBT to Coil and Instrumentation department	
10.	Clearly define the system write up	
11.	Provide heat balance diagram for equipment design to the production units	
12.	Supply equipment parameters to the production unit	
13.	Send the specific requirement, if any, of the customer to production units	
14.	Release scheme for mechanical piping	
15.	Submit piping schedules, valve schedules and heat balance diagram to mechanical piping unit	
16.	Take care of drain and vents	
17.	Change the schemes as per piping layout requirement	
18.	Finalize electric load for electric department	
19.	Furnish the required rating of equipment to electrical department	
20.	Provide the requirements of DM and service water to mechanical auxiliary department	

Sl. No.	Competencies for P and IDS	Type
21.	Carry out preventive maintenance	
22.	Make arrangement for updating the data bank	
23.	Help in diagnosing faults and removal of virus as and when required by computer department	

12. Competencies for Commercial

Sl. No.	Competencies for commercial	Type
1.	Ensure product quality and product prices	
2.	Adhere to time schedules	
3.	Provide effective after sales services	
4.	Train customers to use the product	
5.	Make arrangements for liquidation of age old outstandings	
6.	Ensure that established tendering and other processes are adhered	
7.	Receive advice from others to reduce cost of product	
8.	Make timely collection of sale proceeds	
9.	Provide detailed specification and drawings to production department in time	
10.	Make arrangements for required materials and machines for production department	
11.	Inform production department regarding quantity to be produced	
12.	Give sufficient time to meet the delivery schedule	
13.	Inform the mode of dispatch to supplier and sub-contractors	
14.	Provide time schedule to purchase department for procurement of material	
15.	Provide the quantity of material along with specifications to be purchased by purchase department well in time.	
16.	Provide required specification and tolerances to quality control department	
17.	Help in approval of drawings and design	
18.	Ensure coordination with customer	
19.	Provide detailed customer requirement to design department	
20.	Provide the road survey reports	
21.	Provide concerning details	
22.	Inform requirements of spares and materials to be stored well in advance	
23.	Promote team work in working	
24.	Promote effective communication	
25.	Use computers for various purposes	
26.	Require training in recent techniques	

13. Competencies for Finance

Sl. No.	*Competencies for Finance*	*Type*
1.	Ensure that all personal payments are attended promptly as per rules and regulation	
2.	Prepare plan of activities for smooth functioning	
3.	Prepare realistic budget and try to achieve the milestone	
4.	Develop cordial relations with bankers, customer and other departments	
5.	Adhere to the policies of company	
6.	Ensure timely submission of reports.	
7.	Ensure employees participation for achievement of company's objective	
8.	Honour the commitments with bank guarantee's approval	
9.	Maintain proper books with sanctions, for the auditors.	
10.	Receive payments/collections/invoicing as per budget from headquarters	
11.	Send feedback to headquarters	
12.	Invoice with customer according to conditions/work done	
13.	Obtain suggestions and clarifications from group heads	
14.	Make bill payments in time	
15.	Provide sufficient credit period	
16.	Provide feedback of payments to suppliers	
17.	Coordinate in tender documents and getting of proposal	
18.	Use computers for various activities	
19.	Give satisfactory answers to queries	
20.	Promote team spirit	
21.	Provide clear instructions regarding finance	
22.	Train other related persons on finance management	

14. Competencies for Range Officer

Sl. No.	*Competencies for Range Officer*	*Type*
1.	Develop relationship with villagers to enhance their participation	
2.	Communicate government projects, schemes and policies to the villagers	
3.	Design appropriate participatory rural appraisal tools and techniques to formulate village development projects	
4.	Diagnose current situation of the village	
5.	Prepare simple village and forest development plans involving stakeholders and villagers	
6.	Evolve role of working groups to implement the development plans	
7.	Mobilize local and government resources for implementing the plans	

Sl. No.	*Competencies for Range Officer*	*Type*
8.	Solve problems and take decisions for forest management	
9.	Report the progress to superiors	
10.	Manage information of the range	
11.	Manage conflict	
12.	Investigate the cases of forest theft	
13.	Monitor the progress of government schemes	
14.	Contribute in implementation of schemes of other departments	
15.	Involve non-government organizations in project management	
16.	Impart training to subordinate	
17.	Implement forest laws	
18.	Influence villagers to use alternative sources of energy	
19.	Put up the cases in court of law	
20.	Prepare cases of compensation	
21.	Contribute in research studies	

Glossary

Appraisal : It is an interactive process of identifying the strengths and accordingly setting the goals and preparing the plans to use the strengths.

Accountability : The answerability of employees to management for achieving the individual and organizational goals.

Benchmarking : It is a process of setting the competencies and proficiency for a role with reference to best in that area. Generally, it is used for standard setting.

Career Planning : It involves efforts on the part of the organization to provide adequate opportunities at right time for growth and development of the employees in areas of their interest. The career paths are decided in core areas of the business such as planning, operation, customer care, maintenance, research and development, human résources development, finance management, marketing, counseling, etc.

Competency Assessment : It is the process of collecting authentic evidences with reference to performance on defined competencies for various purposes such as finding gap in competency and proficiency, identifying the potential, measuring the progress of learning and so on.

Competency Framework : The competency framework for an organization is a bundle of competencies derived from the vision, missions, goals, vision reach strategies, values, policies, norms, ethics, strengths, weaknesses, opportunities, resources, major achievements etc. in order to know the nature of human resources required to carry out the business effectively and efficiently.

Competency Mapping : It is about identifying preferred behaviours and personal skills which distinguish excellent and outstanding performance from average. It is a process of identifying key competencies for a particular position in an organization, and then using it for job evaluation, recruitment, training, and development, performance management succession planning etc. [Bhattacharya, 2007]

Competency Profile : It is a set of all types of competencies required to perform a particular role effectively and efficiently in present and near future which contributes significantly for achieving objectives related to core business of the organization.

Competency : The competency is a 'statement which describes the integrated demonstration of a cluster of related knowledge, skills, and attitudes that are observable and measurable, necessary to perform a role independently at a prescribed proficiency level'.

Core Competence : It is the capacity and capability of the organization to achieve the unique and different goals in competitive environment in successful manner at comparatively less cost, time, and efforts. It provides competitive leverage to the organization to deal with external environment.

Continuous Improvement : It is the concept used in total quality management and other philosophy of management. It emphasizes that there should be improvement in the quality of products and services after completion of every cycle of performance. Considering the versatility of concept it is used for every management function like goal setting, process design, performance, etc.

Compensation : It is monetary value provided to employees in exchange of their performance to achieve the goals of the organization.

Counseling : It is a psychological process to identify the behavioural problems of individuals and groups which are detrimental to business of the organization. The individuals are psychologically guided to remain abstain from such behaviour and perform according to set rules, norms and regulations.

Delight : This term is used to express the behaviour of the customers, beneficiaries and clients when they are served more than their genuine expectations.

Development : It is a process of identifying the needs, potential, ambitions and harnessing the same through education, training and practice for the satisfaction of the self and growth and development of the organization.

Effectiveness : It is related to setting right goals. In mathematical terms, it is expressed as actual output divided by planned output.

Efficiency : It is an engineering concept. In mathematical terms, it is expressed as output divided by input.

Enrichment : It is related to creating variety of opportunities for employees to use core competency in performing the role.

Fast Learners : It is the inherent characteristic of the employee to learn new and different concepts, principles, theory and process. They are more attentive, intelligent, vigilant and cautious about the changes taking place in the environment around.

Feedback : The process of receiving information about the behaviour, progress on achievement of goals, quality of performance and method of performance. The information is received from various reliable sources and progress of the work.

Goals : These are the well defined quantitative and qualitative milestones for the organization, departments, teams and individuals for which they put their energy to reach the set destination.

Human Resources Development: It is a process of continuously improving the competence, capability and capacity of employees of the organisation using proactive approaches of awareness, education, training and development endeavours.

HR Processes : All processes designed, implemented and evaluated to manage the employees of the organization. These processes are designed by HR managers and implemented by all managers.

Incentives : It is a kind of recognition provided to employees for their performance up to the mark or more than that.

Innovation : It is a process of implementing creative ideas to achieve unique, different, novel and most desired objectives with minimum efforts, time and available resources.

Job Planning : The Jobs or roles of individuals and teams are decided on the basis of vision reach strategies, competence and interest so that all the activities of the organization can be implemented effectively and efficiently. At the same time the individuals are also satisfied by their performance.

Job Rotation : The individuals are shifted from one position to another similar position after a certain period of time for various reasons such as breaking the monotony, developing the person for performing similar jobs, and providing opportunity to other persons.

Mission : The most desirous vision of the organization is achieved using mission statements in core areas of business derived from the vision of the organization. Mission statements express long-term milestones of development of the organization. These statements are useful in designing alternative strategies for development and influencing the stakeholders for extending guidance and support. The mission statements act as a source of encouragement for employees.

Motivational Climate : The meaning of the motivational climate is related to inner urge to demonstrate the behaviour individually and collectively that is aligned to reaching the vision of the organization. Organizational members are self-motivated to achieve day-to-day results keeping long-term objectives and goals in mind. Their energy is channelized and guided by the objectives they have in mind that are aligned to purposeful vision and mission of the institute. In many situations individuals and groups working in the institution become the source of motivation for each other. They spark the urge to do better for the institution.

Organizational Development : It is a process of diagnosing the current functioning of the organization in the light of expected performance and developing the human resources and other systems in order to achieve excellence.

Obtrusive Observation : It is a kind of observation made of performance of the individuals against well defined criteria in natural setting without informing the individuals.

Potential : The personal capacity and capability of individuals and groups for achieving specific goals without much of efforts.

Proactive : It is a concept related to anticipating, visualizing, and predicting the future scenario based on limited information related to business to set the goals and design the strategies to achieve the same in planned manner.

Professional Approach : It is a process of proactively performing in the organization assuring quality of product and services without any waste of time, efforts, money and energy and providing the goods and services at right time in right quantity to customers.

Professionals : These are the individuals and teams who perform in effective and efficient manner to achieve the organizational goals and objectives. Along with technical competencies they demonstrate professional competencies such as accepting the challenge, risk taking, working in a team, quick learning, problem solving, effective decision making, negotiating, collaborating, networking, working in uncertainty, predicting the future, visualizing the whole on the basis of available data, accepting accountability, managing change, coping with situation, influencing the customer, undertaking research and projects for quick response, adjusting in new environment and new culture, learning new and different competencies, forgetting fast, and so on. These competencies are different for different professions.

Proficiency : It is related to expected standard of performance and behaviour with reference to core business, quality of products and services, rules and regulations, working practices and processes of the organization.

Personality : It refers to the organized, consistent, and general pattern of behaviour of a person which helps her/him to understand her/his behaviour as an individual.

Perspective Planning : It is a process of setting 3 to 5 years goals and designing strategies to achieve the same.

Policy : It is a broad statement that guides the decision making process or actions in the organization.

Responsive : The organization identifies the changing needs of the customers and accordingly produces products and offers services to always satisfy the customers. It also predicts the internal and external requirements related to production and accordingly reorganizes the processes.

Role Dimensions : These are various aspects of role in which the position holders perform to satisfy the expectations of others and self. For example, a professor performs on various role dimensions such as teaching, learning resources development, research, consultancy, publication, curriculum design, assessment, administration, guidance and counseling and so on.

Role : The employees fulfil the expectations of the internal and external members in the organization performing various tasks. The behaviour exhibited by the employees during the performance is called role.

Role Significance : The important position assigned to a person in the organization is liked by that person and people get influenced by the performance of the person.

Role Enrichment : The role of the person is designed in such a way so that there is an opportunity for holding significant position, using variety of competency possessed, and freedom to plan the performance goals and implement strategies with a provision of internal as well as external feedback on the performance.

Redeployment : The business of organizations is continuously changing in order to grab external opportunity for the growth and development of the organization. In changing environment the competencies and even manpower requirements at all levels may not match with the requirements of the core business. It is social responsibility of the organization to provide sustained employment to its employees. In such situations the existing employees are trained to develop new competencies which are needed to perform the changing business. These trained employees are redeployed for new role.

Self Development : It is a systematic and conscious process of identifying the needs, creating opportunities, and extending facilities to undergo various learning programmes for enhancing the ability, capability, competency, proficiency and commitment for excelling better for the benefit of the organization.

Satisfaction : This term is used to express the behaviour of the employees when they get what they expect in terms of monetary, social and psychological rewards.

Stakeholders : The individuals and groups who influence the performance of employees in the organization or the employee can influence their performance.

Standards : The quantitative and qualitative values related to competencies and proficiency against which assessment and comparison is made.

Strategic Goals : The long-term milestones the organization wants to achieve in order to achieve missions and vision of the organization.

Strategic Plan : It is written document prepared by every organization after going through rigorous planning exercises. It is prepared for 10 to 20 years. It is very broad in nature. It contains vision, missions, goals, and alternative strategies to accomplish vision of the organization. It provides base for preparing perspective and annual plans. It acts as a foundation for further planning process. The soundness of the strategic plan decides the future of the organization.

Succession Planning : It is a process of ensuring availability of right person for right role at any particular time for ensuring sustenance and development of the business. It also includes the process of identifying, training and developing people to assume higher responsibility.

Self Actualization : It is the highest level of development of the individual.

Self Concept : It is the own assessment of individual about herself/ himself in a particular context.

The Training Needs : These are defined in two contexts. First, it is defined in present context as the gaps in competency and proficiency level of the individual/team because of that they are not able to perform their role effectively and efficiently to meet performance standards although necessary resources required to perform the role are available in the organization. Second, it is defined in future context as the gaps perceived by the organization in the competency and proficiency level of the individual/team to perform potential roles in the organization. The standard competency profile is used for identifying the training needs.

Total Quality Management : It is a system developed in organization for sustaining, improving and expanding the scope of quality of products and services for satisfying and delighting the customers.

Training : It is an opportunity created by the organization for its employees to develop themselves to self-actualization level in order to harness and use their full potential for the development of the organization and derive satisfaction out of it. It is imparted formally and informally to empower people to perform proficiently.

Value Addition : The systematic and scientific methods are used to enhance the quality of products and services of the organization. The value is added at input level, process level and output level to delight the customers and make them cheerful. Various methods, media and information technology are used to add the value at each stage of functioning of the organization. Various methods such as suggestions, creativity, interview and common sense are used for adding value to products and services.

Values : Values serve as the foundation of relationship and the work for the organization. Values guide the work and relationship in the organization. These are expressed in terms of excellence, quality, concerns, customer satisfaction, community services, and commitment to contribute for new technology, self-development and so on.

Vision : It is the statement of future intents of organization that the organization wants to achieve in planned and professional manner. It is expressed in future expectations of the customers and employees. It sets the aspirations and ambitions of the employees. It provides the clear picture of the destination of the organization. It is always stated in positive and enduring terms. It bridges the gap between present and future. Many organizations are expressing it in quality and value loaded terms. The vision is never constrained by current limitations, capabilities, and capacities of the organization.

Vision Reach Strategies : The organization, groups and individuals design a broad framework of efforts, resources and time to achieve the crafted vision.

Summary

This book is a guide for development of competency framework and management of human resources. This book contains 9 self-explanatory chapters with ample figures, models, guidelines, tools, techniques, formats, and activities. Glossary of terms and frequently asked questions are other special features of this book.

Chapter 1 describes the concept, features, classification and sources of competency with examples.

Chapter 2 highlights the concept, need, importance, and use of competency framework. It also describes the characteristics and factors affecting competency framework.

Chapter 3 describes the models of competency framework, concept of competency profile and competency map and guidelines for developing competency framework.

Chapter 4 describes the organizational diagnosis, review and information gathering tools and techniques for developing and using competency framework.

Chapter 5 explains the concept, characteristics and types of assessment. It explains factors affecting assessment, process of involving stakeholders and paradigm shift required in assessment.

Chapter 6 explains process of competency based recruitment, tools, techniques and issues involved in recruitment.

Chapter 7 provides overview of competency based training that describes the concept, benefits, and model of competency based training. It emphasizes the shift required from content oriented training to competency based training.

Chapter 8 describes the emerging concepts of performance appraisal, use of competency for organizational planning and performance planning, and decisions based on various types of assessment.

Chapter 9 describes the role, behaviour and competency profile of HR managers.

At the end of the book answers of frequently asked questions related to competency framework and human resources management are given from real life situation.

Bibliography

Bhattacharya, Shubhasheesh (2007). Competency Mapping: Concepts and Practices, *Business Manager*, Vol. 10. No. 5, [November 2007]

Boyatzis, R. E. (1982). *The Competent Manager: A Model for Effective Performance*, John Wiley, New York, NY.

Byham, W. C. (1996). Assessment centers, the place for packing management potential, in *European Business*, Brussels, Autumn.

Byham, W. C. (1996). *Developing Dimension—Competency-based Human Resource Systems*, Development Dimensions International.

Cook, Kevin W. and Bernthal, Paul (1998). *Job/Role Competency Practices Survey Report*, Development Dimensions International.

Finch, Curtis R. & Crunkilton, John R. (1979). *Curriculum Development in Vocational and Technical Education*, Allyn and Bacon Inc., Boston.

Finch, Curtis R. & Crunkilton, John R. (1989). *Competency-Based Education in Curriculum Development in Vocational and Technical Education,* Boston: Allyn and Bacon, (3rd Ed.).

Finch, Curtis R. & Crunkilton, John R. (1993). *Curriculum Development in Vocational and Technical Education – Planning, Content and Implementation.* Boston: Allyn and Bacon Inc.

Gupta (2007). *Management of Competency Based Learning*, Concept Publishing Company Pvt. Ltd., New Delhi.

Gupta, (2007). *Management of Competency Based Training and Education*, Quality Publishing Company, Bhopal.

Gupta, B. L. & Anil Kumar (2009). *Entrepreneurship Development*, Mahamaya Publishing Company, New Delhi.

Gupta, B. L. & Joshua Earnest (2008). *Competency Based Curriculum*, Mahamaya Publishing Company, New Delhi.

Klemp, G.O. Jr. (1980). *The Assessment of Occupational Competence*. Report to the National Institute of Education, Washington, DC.

Lewis, Roger (1995). Competence-based Learning at the University of Humberside. U.K. Employment Department Sheffield, *Journal of Competence and Assessment*, Issue 30.

Marshall, Patricia (1996). Why are some people more successful than others? in *People and Competencies*, edited by Nick Boulter, Murray Dalziel and Jackie Hill, Kogan Page, Second Edition.

Maxwell, G.W. *et al.* (1980). *Handbook for California Vocational Educators*. US: San Jose State University, California; Microfiche No. ED 210 518.

Model and Method of Competency Mapping and Assessment, Sunrise Model, Mumbai.

Nick Boulter, Murray Dalziel & Jackie Hill (2004), *People and Competencies, A Handbook*, Crest Publishing House, New Delhi.

Race, Phil (2005). *Making Learning Happen,* Sage Publications.

Rankin, N. (2004). The new prescription for performance: the eleventh competency benchmarking survey, *Competency & Emotional Intelligence Benchmarking, 2004-05*, IRS (Lexis Nexus UK), 2004.

Sanghi, Seema (2007). *The Handbook of Competency Mapping*, Response Books, New Delhi.

Soni, S. K. (1997). Competence-based Technician Education. New Delhi: *The Indian Journal of Technical Education*; Vol. 20, No. 2.

Widest, Steve & Hollywood (2004). *A Practical Guide to Competencies*, Jaico Publishing House, Mumbai.

Index